Helping Yourself
with
Psycho-Cosmic Power

Helping Yourself
with
Psycho-Cosmic Power

Al G. Manning, D.D.

Parker Publishing Company, Inc.
West Nyack, New York

PRINTED IN THE UNITED STATES OF AMERICA

B & P

Dedication

To Professor Reinhardt and the other "unseen" helpers

What This Book Can Do
for You

A few "lucky" people seem to be swept along to greater and greater success, happiness, and fulfillment of their desires. They demonstrate a fantastic ability to *accomplish*, because they are tapping a stream of irresistible energy! This same energy flows largely unharnessed through the lives of all of us, just waiting to be used. You have only to recognize its value, reach out, and *use it!*

The evolution of the harnessing of our country's natural resources provides many good examples. For centuries, the mighty Colorado River flowed peacefully through the Western United States, emptying its energy and substance into the sea. Then the intelligence of man recognized the great potential going to waste, and Hoover Dam (or Boulder Dam if you prefer) was built. The dam transforms the Colorado's potential into the energy that lights many cities, and into the irrigation that grows abundant crops where there was only desert before.

What psycho-cosmic power can do for you

A tremendous stream of creative-psychic energy flows through your being, carrying a greater potential force for you than a mighty river carries for its own valley. This Psycho-Cosmic Power (we will call it PCP in this book) in you is just waiting—waiting for you to build your personal "Hoover Dam" and reap its fantastic material, financial, psychic, and spiritual benefits! This book presents a series of practical methods, organized in a space-age approach to achieving your personal success and effectiveness through PCP (Psycho-Cosmic Power). We will adopt the general philosophy that you should use *anything that works or helps you,* regardless of the origin or background of the idea or technique. Therefore, we will borrow techniques from modern science, the aerospace industry, psychology, metaphysics, the mystery schools, occult folklore, and plain old "common sense." Our only test of an idea's validity will be, *"Will it work for you?"*

Would you like to be a highly successful business executive? An accomplished author? An artist? Teacher? Then shall we add personal magnetism and perfect health? And peace of mind together with a new personal relationship to God, Cosmic Good? Any or all of these—your heart's own special desire—can be yours when you master PCP.

Mastery of PCP means complete control over the causes that manifest themselves as your total life expression, including your health, finances, security, and significant accomplishments. The purpose of this book is to guide and program your progress toward the attainment of effective control of PCP, and thus, of your life's greatest expression. The few "lucky" people demonstrate a wonderful degree of control over their lives, while the teeming mass of humanity struggles desperately for little more than daily survival. It's obviously worth making the effort to lift yourself up out of the frustrating struggle and into the "special" or "lucky" category. You will find that each successive step up from the depths of the struggle brings its own reward, and is completely worthwhile for its own sake. But, woven into a careful pattern, these small steps can lead you ever upward to heights of accomplishment that exist beyond the limits of your present thinking.

This book is planned for your use

Since I am an *active* student of life—not a scholar—this book is written for those active people who learn by *applying* new ideas to their everyday life situations. This is the secret of all progress! The language and examples used are simple because I believe that simple things and ideas are the only ones worth our effort to understand—there are no complex ideas, only complex explanations of basically simple ideas.

This book sets up ways that you can demonstrate the usefulness of Universal Cosmic Truths *by their practical application* to any problem in your life. The final results are up to you! You are entitled to expression, fulfillment, accomplishment, and complete control of all areas of your life. You now have the power in your hands, with this book, to use the Cosmic Forces to order your life to your complete satisfaction.

AL G. MANNING

Contents

periences in astral travel. Now you know you can exist apart from your physical body. How to tap the wisdom of the ages. How a practical spirit helped a hairdresser. Your first simple steps to spirit contact. Points to remember from this chapter.

Popularity adds zest to your life. How to build your launch pad to ever greater popularity. How to use PCP to increase your personal magnetism. How to renew your personal magnetism. How to handle special personalities. How to enjoy close friendships with PCP. How to improve rapport with all people. Points to remember from this chapter.

Let's not be bound by old clichés. My own experience in marriage using PCP. How to build your launch pad to a perfect companionship. How to be ready to attract your perfect mate. How to handle the courtship period. How to insure a long-term happy marriage. Points to remember from this chapter.

You are on earth to express the magnificence of Cosmic Deity. How to build your launch pad to freedom from limitation. How PCP disposed of an impossible marital situation. Using PCP to break stalemated conditions.

how to

Transform Your Wishes and Dreams into Psycho-Cosmic Power (PCP)

Modern man rushes toward greater and greater scientific accomplishment, confident that he is gaining control over his world. He exhibits a nearly blind faith in his rockets and lasers, his complex computers and electronically controlled machines. He seems to think they will soon give him total comfort and complete mastery of his environment—and perhaps mastery of the whole universe.

Science and industry are bringing us many useful gadgets. But what good is a three dimensional color television set if you can't meet the payments? Or a million dollars in the bank if you are in the last stages of a killer disease? Or perfect health when you can't find a job? Our real need is the *personal power* to accomplish our goals and improve our station in life.

By intelligent application of your own infinite supply of Psycho-Cosmic Power (PCP), you can achieve unlimited improvement in every area of your life. No reasonable human being can afford to ignore this most potent of all forces.

What is Psycho-Cosmic Power?

The unbelievably effective force that flows in and through your being has been known in part by effective men since the dawn of time. In various of its aspects it has been called nerve energy, psychic energy, thought power, spirit energy, magnetism, subconscious power, or just plain enthusiasm. But it is much more than all of these! When you are attuned to the stream of psychic-nerve-magnetic-thought-light-enthusiasm-spirit energy which is expressing as your being, your properly conceived desire becomes the positive desire of the Universe—and *nothing can prevent its manifestation!* There seems to be no better name for this irresistible energy than PSYCHO-COSMIC POWER. (We will regularly abbreviate this as PCP.)

Like the majestic Colorado River before the great dam was built, the potential of PCP in each of us is largely wasted. But whatever we do accomplish is a direct result of our use of PCP, whether we use it consciously or unconsciously. Obviously it is to our very best interest to study this energy with an eye to learning to control it in all of its many aspects.

Let's dig into PCP a little deeper. The very life energy which animates your fleshly body is an aspect of PCP, but so is the substance of your body. In its grossest forms we call it *matter*, and in higher forms *energy*. Electricity and magnetism are important forms of PCP because they are easily studied for clues as to the basic nature of the primordial energy-substance and the curiously complex simplicity of its laws of action. Sound and light are even more important forms of PCP because we can use them to exercise new and startling control over its manifestations. We will pause to take a broad look at the whole spectrum of PCP. If we were to draw an illustrative line from the grossest form of PCP to the finest, it would look like this:

MATTER-ENERGY-EMOTION-THOUGHT-SOUL-SPIRIT-INFINITY

It is important to understand that this line is continuous and unbroken. Science has conclusively proved that matter and energy are convertible into one another. But this is only one little part of the lower end of our spectrum, and the shading from each form of PCP to the next, all along the line, is smooth and without any trace of a crack, bump, or break. As we unfold the intricacies of working with Psycho-Cosmic Power, we will see that this continuity of expression, from common matter all the way to infinity, is the key to the success of our every undertaking.

Looking back at our illustrative line, you will notice that emotion and thought form the central section of all expression. Thus we see that control of the sum total of our existence is attainable as we first control our thoughts and emotions, then extend this mastery in both directions. We will learn to use PCP to function effectively on the material as well as the mental, psychic, and spirit levels. And at the right time, we will be able to reach out and contact infinity itself.

PCP can be tapped to provide an infinite source of power and energy, and make it available to you on an "as needed" basis. Anything you want for a constructive purpose can be manifested easily through the simple process of turning on the flow of Psycho-Cosmic Power. The nature of PCP is to be constructive or evolutionary in its method of manifesting—it changes conditions or builds material things by apparently natural growth processes. *Psycho-Cosmic power accomplishes real miracles* in the lives of normal people every day. Isn't it time *you* learned to cash in on this infinite bounty?

Three simple steps to control of PCP

Our starting point is the simple statement of the basic formula for creation by the use of PCP:

Your properly formed desire, reinforced by sound and creative imagination, attracts the cosmic power of manifestation.

You may be feeling doubt right now, but we will demonstrate to you that this formula is packed with enough power to light the whole world. It will certainly bring the light of happiness, prosperity, health, and joy into your life—*if you give it a chance!*

The three simple steps to using the PCP formula for creation are:

1. *Tune your consciousness to the PCP frequency.*

This can be simply compared to radio communication. It is necessary to generate a carrier wave on a chosen frequency, and provide enough power to carry your message to the receiving station. Our object is to generate a Psycho-Cosmic Power carrier wave, and give it the power to reach the receiving station of the Infinite.

2. *Express your desire in terms of PCP.*

Continuing our analogy of radio communication, it is necessary to modulate the carrier wave with the natural vibrations of the message itself. We will learn to modulate your PCP carrier wave with the details of your properly constructed desire.

3. *Push the PCP "start button."*

Then leave the results to the infinite power and intelligence of the Cosmic. Once you set the PCP forces in motion, your desire has become the desire of the Cosmic Itself, and nothing can prevent its manifestation.

Now we will turn our attention to the "how" of using infinite PCP energies.

How to tune your consciousness to the PCP frequency

The Gospel according to St. John, though generally called the mystical gospel, hides a very practical method of producing our PCP carrier wave. Let's look at a bit of the opening chapter: *In the beginning was the Word, and the Word was with God, and the Word was God. . . . And the Word was made flesh, and dwelt among us. . . .*

We will leave the ecclesiastical meaning to the religionists and concentrate only on what can be learned of a strictly practical and secular nature. The term *Word* gives us our clue that the carrier wave is somehow connected with sound. Most religions base their methods of contacting Deity on some form of ritual which includes chanting, singing, or the use of a mantra (mystic incantation). The mystical union of desire with the power of ritual sound produces a very strong force which is believed to reach the "ear" of the Deity being invoked.

Yes, a practical man would scoff at this point. But after a little honest experimentation, your scoff will turn to astonishment. To build our carrier wave we will choose that most powerful of all chants, the Mystic Mantra of the Orient. It is *Om, mane padme, hum,* rendered slowly as a melodic chant.

"OM" is from the same root as the English *amen,* and is pronounced like *aum.* It is considered the most mystical of all words because it starts at the deepest point of the throat (the "ahh" sound) and finishes with the lips closing in the "mmmm" sound. Thus "om" is verbally symbolic of the Alpha and Omega, the beginning and the end. "MANE" is pronounced "ma" (as in mama) and "ne" (as in knee). "PADME" is "pa" (as in papa) and "me" (rhyming with knee). "HUM" is really another form of "om" and rhymes with it.

A rough translation might be: *Om, jewel of the lotus, Om.*

The spiritual significance is obvious when we remember that the lotus is the Oriental symbol of ultimate spiritual enlightenment.

The mantra should be rendered slowly, using one very deep breath. Keep the first "om" syllable going for about half the breath, then the "mane padme," and draw out the "hum." Thus:

Ommmmmmmmmmmmmmmmmmmmmmm, mane padme, hummmmmmm.

Practice intoning the phrase a few times to get the feel of the words and rhythm. Learn to enjoy the sound of your voice as you chant the phrase, "Om, mane padme, hum," and concentrate on attaining a feeling of oneness with the Cosmic. Plan to spend fifteen minutes twice a day using the mystic phrase and claiming your attunement with the geat PCP energy of the universe. If you faithfully carry out this process, you will receive an unmistakable response from the Cosmic within two or three weeks. Then continue regular use of the mantra to build and maintain this personal contact with the source of all the power of the universe.

As you sit chanting the mantra and seeking, you will experience an ever growing feeling of complete oneness with the power behind all creation—you will feel all the power of the universe flowing through your being. When you reach this point, you have created your PCP carrier wave. It is none other than that feeling of oneness with the Source of All Power.

How to express your desires in terms of PCP

We described our next step as modulating the carrier wave. This is accomplished by mixing your desire with the feeling of oneness with the universe. Naturally some things mix more readily than others. For example, water and alcohol mix easily, but water and oil will not mix of their own volition. If we wish to mix water and oil, we must use an emulsifying agent and agitation, or some type of chemical catalyst.

We can safely generalize that things mix readily when they are compatible in nature, and not otherwise. The basic method of mixing your desire with the PCP carrier wave is to make sure that the desire is compatible with the basic nature of the Cosmic. Simple compatibility means that your desire is in harmony with the underlying creative, loving givingness of the life-sustaining PCP force. We may say that a minimum standard for simple compatibility is the fulfillment of the condition that *the fulfillment of this particular desire will be good for you, and will hurt no other person.*

Let's look at a few desires which will require some sort of "mental emulsifier" before they can be mixed with the PCP carrier wave. The urge to steal or to harm a fellow being would fall into this category. There are people who practice techniques whereby they "trick" the PCP energy into doing their negative bidding, but this falls into a class of actions we might call "black magic." Although they may seem to "get away with it" for a time, the eventual price paid by the "black magician" is far more than anyone can afford. Therefore I will give absolutely no instruction in black magic. However we will find it useful to study our desires and thus learn the ways we can safely and honestly make them compatible with the givingness of the Psycho-Cosmic Power.

The great goal of the Cosmic is its own expression through each one of us as an individual. It seeks to express those marvelous qualities of love, effectiveness, intelligence, compassion, abundance, and joy which remain only potential and abstract until the PCP power can bring them into the life of some individual being. Anything that brings you more life, beauty, happiness, unfoldment, accomplishment, love, expression, and joy is just what the infinite PCP force yearns to bring you. Your personal desires are derived from the basic giving-ness of the Cosmic as it is directed toward you, and they are completely pure and wholesome in nature. But because we are more or less blinded by the pressures and customs of our immediate social and economic environment, we often con-fuse or distort the basically good urges coming to us from "on high." Then we may think we want something specific which might bring harm to another or even block our own spiritual growth. Negative desires are always our distortion of a whole-some urge directed to us by the Cosmic.

For example: one of the parties to a very unhappy marriage may honestly feel that the only solution is the death of the other partner. Then in unguarded moments, he (or she) may actually *desire* the death of the spouse. We know without hesitation that the specific expression of this desire is wrong! But if we back up and look at the broader, general desire behind it, we will find the very wholesome yearning for free-dom from tension in the home, for pleasant companionship, love, financial plenty, and happiness. It is quite proper to use your PCP to attain these things, but only in ways which will bring the highest good to all persons involved in the situation.

After seven years of marriage, a young executive began to realize that the reason for his general feeling of unhappiness was the tremendous tension in his home. Careful study showed that he and his wife had very little in common when they married, and had grown steadily apart ever since. He had three fine children, a comfortable five-figure income, and an appar-ently bright future; but he was utterly miserable. He professed to be staying married only for the sake of the children, but a "psychic reading" showed otherwise. Then he admitted he felt that the children would be much better off if the tension were removed from the home by his departure, but he was trapped by a double fear—fear of loneliness, and fear of financial dis-comfort. He was then able to prepare a PCP PERT Chart, as we will learn to do in Chapter 3, and he soon reached an amicable settlement with his wife. They are both happily married now, but each to a partner of more compatible taste and temperament.

Another young man in a rather menial clerical position dreamed of business and financial success. He organized a plan to apply PCP to his business career and succeeded in doubling his income each year for four complete cycles. By then he felt comfortable enough to turn his attention to spiritual progression as a means of balancing his life expression. This was accomplished by applying PCP to the broad desire for success and the highest good for all. In the process, he helped his company double its volume in nearly the same cycle as that of his own financial progress.

But perhaps the most satisfying triumphs are those of the many people whose specific desires for alcohol, drugs, or promiscuous sexual activity have been generalized to the seeking of deeper spiritual growth. No matter what your specific desire, or how negative or ridiculous it seems, it can be backed up to a broad natural desire that is wholesome and life giving in its fulfillment. Only then is it safe to apply your PCP with fervor and energy, and *achieve your goal!*

Now modulate the carrier wave, and let the Cosmic potential build up

When you feel your desire is sufficiently generalized, it is time to transmit it to the great source of all Psycho-Cosmic Power. Begin by tuning your consciousness to the PCP frequency. Use the mantra until you feel your special oneness with all the power of the universe. Then express your desire in your own words, out loud, to the Cosmic. Repeat it over and over in that feeling of oneness, until you feel it passing over and becoming a desire of the Universe Itself.

The process may take ten seconds, ten minutes, several hours, or perhaps days. Keep working with the PCP force until you know deep within your being that your desire has blended with the PCP carrier wave and become truly a Cosmic desire. No one can describe the sensation in words, but it is *real*, and you will *know* when you have succeeded.

At this happy point, you are ready to push the PCP "start button."

Points to Remember from This Chapter

1. The most potent force in the universe is Psycho-Cosmic Power (PCP).

2. Most people waste their PCP power because they don't use it.

3. The three simple steps to controlling PCP are:
    (1) Tune your consciousness to the PCP frequency.
    (2) Express your desire in terms of PCP.
    (3) Push the PCP "start button."

4. Use the mystic mantra, *"Om, mane padme, hum,"* to tune your consciousness to the PCP frequency.

5. You can express your desires in terms of PCP by working back to the wholesome, natural urge back of each specific desire.

6. Make your desire a Cosmic Desire by repeating your purified request while in PCP attunement.

how to
Push the PCP
"Start" Button

An old hunting rifle barks out its missile toward the selected target, but only when someone pulls its trigger. In the first two steps of the PCP formula we have loaded, and then aimed our PCP rifle. Now let's think about pulling the trigger, or as we put it before, pushing the "start" button.

It's like launching a rocket

The best analogy to PCP firing is the now familiar procedure of launching a rocket, as for a space probe. Months, and even years, before the firing button is pushed, plans and preparations have been falling into place along a logical timetable. First the goal or target end result must be specifically agreed upon. Here the present "state of the art" is considered, and plotted against the obvious requirements for the success of the mission being conceived.

Within the various technologies which both make possible and limit the space program, our scientists and engineers have learned to extrapolate from historical rates of progress. Thus it was possible to say with some degree of confidence in the early 1960's that we would put a man on the moon by 1970, and bring him back as well. Such significant accomplishments are the result of carefully coordinated effort. Tremendous tasks involving thousands of scientists and engineers, supported by other thousands of technicians and production workers, are broken down into minute subtasks which are manageable by individuals or small groups. Then PERT planning techniques allow sophisticated computers to maintain regular periodic monitoring of over-all task progress by analyzing data from the tiny operating groups. Thus projects are flagged as requiring special attention to keep from slipping behind schedule, and careful evaluations are made of the effects of schedule variations of small task segments on the timetable for the program as a whole.

But we have been considering only the mental phase. While all this fancy planning and computer monitoring goes on, somebody must be supplying the physical and technological needs of the program. Ideas must be translated into equations, drawings, and finally into the millions of bits of hardware that eventually get assembled as the space vehicle itself or, of equal importance, as the launching gear and telemetry and monitoring equipment. This enormous array of hardware will finally acquire the new knowledge that is our excuse for undertaking the program in the first place.

Now we enter the critical period, the last few hours before the scheduled blast off. Here the PERT Charts give way to the detailed countdown procedure. But in a broader sense, countdown is merely a specialized form of PERT. In these last few hours, everything that has gone before, all of the detailed preparations, must be checked and double checked. And yet, this is not so different from planning a weekend vacation. The final minutes before piling the family into the car for the "blast off" are spent in a sort of countdown—"Did you put in bathing suits? Golf clubs? Toothbrushes and toothpaste? How about my slippers? Is the tank full of gasoline? Have the tires been

checked? And what about the spare tire? . . ." You undoubtedly know a family whose countdown before a weekend
trip seems more painstaking than the ones made at a NASA
launching facility for a moonshot.

Finally we reach the magic moment, and it is time to turn
the starter switch or push the firing button. How shall we go
about pushing ours? We have already achieved our oneness
with the source of PCP, and expressed our desire in the proper
terms to have it accepted as a desire of the universe. At this
point in your activity, you feel the PCP potential building up
and up to a peak. Right at this point you can trigger the
process by mentally pushing a button while saying aloud something like, "I now launch my PCP rocket. I release this desire
into the care of the Cosmic, and I know it cannot fail to manifest!"

Then let it go! In your mind's eye, watch your "rocket" take
off toward the source of all Psycho-Cosmic Power. Just as a
space probe is carefully monitored, you can observe the flight
of your desire. In a PCP launch, just as a rocket launch, it is the
first few seconds that are the most critical. The rocket must
achieve full power and break away cleanly from its launch
mechanism, otherwise the mission will be a failure if not a
disaster. Although there is not quite the same danger to your
launching mechanism as to that of a rocket, *the point of launch
is most critical.* Thus it will pay us to concentrate our attention
on the preparations immediately preceding the launch.

The special importance of the countdown

At a NASA countdown, much of the emphasis is on checking
the various safety devices and backup systems for the protection of personnel, the launch area, and the bird itself. In a PCP
shot, the safety angle is to be certain you really want the result
you are seeking. This is the time to double check the adjust-

ment of your desire to compatibility with the Psycho-Cosmic Power.

How a salesman adjusted his countdown

As part of his countdown, a young salesman stopped to re-evaluate his adjusted desire. He had changed it from wishing his sales manager would be fired so he could have the job, to the more wholesome desire that his sales manager would be promoted so he could fill the vacancy. Better, it's true, but it still smacks too much of controlling the lives of other people. Before it was too late, he adjusted his desire again. This time he merely stated, "I desire a new position which will utilize my sales and managerial talents and allow me to expand both in effectiveness and income." Then with a feeling of new safety with his readjusted desire, he pushed his PCP on button. On the third day, his telephone rang and he was invited to lunch to talk about a sales management position in a new division his company was opening. It turned out to be a job that seemed tailor-made to his special abilities, and he was highly successful from almost the first day.

How to conserve your energy for PCP

Another important reason for the laborious countdown is to avoid wasting the expensive rocket. Let's face the simple fact that as long as we occupy the human form we are limited in the amount of time and energy we have available to devote to any activity, even the direction of our PCP. Our work will be much more effective and less disappointing if we prepare properly and so avoid miserable failures.

This brings up another important point. Every once in a while we hear of a NASA mission being scrubbed because of unfavorable weather conditions. All missions designed to visit bodies other than earth are planned to be launched at a time when the target and earth are favorably located in relation to each other. In other words, there are external conditions over which we have no control as well as conditions that we can control. The most important judgment factor a person can develop is the ability to tell the difference. An ardent metaphysician may tell you there is no external condition that cannot be controlled by the mind, but he will back off quickly if you ask him to delay sunrise or the high tide for just four or five hours tomorrow morning.

We must admit that there are some conditions and things which we can control completely, others that we can affect to some extent, and still others that are totally beyond our ability to budge in the slightest. And it is wonderful that this is so! Otherwise some sorehead might just turn off the sun and plunge the whole world into chaos.

A prudent investor would not commit a large portion of his fortune without considering the recent performance of the stock market and his best judgment of the current business cycle. Sometimes it may be necessary to swim upstream, but it might be much better to get out of the water and walk. We are playing with the simple value of *timing*, but let's defer a deeper discussion long enough to look at some special ways of avoiding the waste of your PCP energy.

Avoid wasting your PCP and make every shot count!

It will pay to explore your personal attitude toward PCP. There are two poles of weakness which should be avoided with equal fervor. They are the narrow mindedness of the material-scientific approach, and the starry-eyed impracticality of the naïve metaphysician. Let's take a quick look at the defects of each.

The material-scientific community cheerfully accepts the limitations of time, space, and the present "state of the art." The tremendous struggle that has been necessary to bring some degree of scientific respectability to parapsychology illustrates the major defect of the system. Anything that doesn't fit perfectly into the accepted scheme of things is suspect, and subject to ridicule and derision.

"The state of the art" is almost a god to our engineering community. Although they work constantly to extend this accepted boundary, they cheerfully accept its limitations in the "short run." It clearly resembles the security pattern of children—the need for a clear line past which it is forbidden to venture. The great god they worship is something called "repeatability." If a phenomenon or experiment can be repeated in the laboratory, the men of science and engineering will agree it's true; but any experience which transcends the fund of available knowledge is an "accident" or "coincidence." Unfortunately from the standpoint of the advancement of man's fund of useful knowledge many circumstances in real life cannot be exactly duplicated. Thus it becomes "impossible to prove repeatability."

Would you ask a man who has just been miraculously healed of terminal cancer to submit to his misery again merely to prove repeatability? And what of the cures that don't work? If a "faith healer" fails, he is called a fake or a charlatan. But show me one medical doctor who has never lost a patient!

Similarly, you wouldn't ask a man to quit a very comfortable executive position merely to prove that he can use the laws of PCP to get one that is equal or better. That would no doubt get you into trouble. This type of situation is clearly covered by the oft repeated Biblical injunction, "Thou shalt not tempt the Lord thy God." The prudent will simply forget about repeatability in relation to the universal laws of Psycho-

Cosmic Power. Your only concern is that it works *once—when you need it!* Leave consideration of things like repeatability to the eggheads. Use PCP. It will work every time you need it!

This is not to say that we should let ourselves bog down in a morass of impractical mysticism. There is a state of *mystic attunement with the universe.* It is wonderful for its own sake, and we will learn how to seek it in a later chapter. But the mystic experience alone is of no value in our everyday world of striving and commerce. In the workaday world the Pollyanna attitude of the naïve metaphysician is useless. Of course love and pure motivations are necessary, but the purest of motivations will never cover up for poor judgment.

The good metaphysician prays or "treats" for his desire constantly. His motto is, "Keep on keeping on." But even when he has a successful "demonstration," he may find that he derives no satisfaction from the very thing he spent so much energy to achieve. We are really saying that the metaphysician wastes tremendous amounts of PCP energy by forgetting to start with a careful countdown. I studied and experimented with metaphysics for many years, and have a tremendous respect for its potential. But it is not enough by itself. There is no substitute for the sound judgment that looks at reality and decides what can be changed—then tackles life with a carefully-laid plan which uses PCP with maximum effectiveness.

But how do you decide what you are capable of changing? We will do much toward developing that judgment with a careful study of the value of timing.

The tremendous value of timing for PCP

When a great ship runs aground, men make careful preparations for its rescue. Much work will be done on preliminaries, but the actual attempt to refloat the vessel can come only at high tide. Seafarers of all nations have learned to blend their efforts with the natural forces of the universe. Their regular use of tides, wind and stars is an excellent example of the positive use of timing. We are reminded of this in the timeworn saying, "Time and tide wait for no man."

You can change any condition in your life if your timing is right! But if you insist on bucking the universal tide, you may struggle vainly for months or years, and then be too worn out to be effective when the right time presents itself. The true secret of success is in conserving your PCP energies for currently practical projects. It isn't easy to tell just where it is most practical to apply your energies at any given moment. So people have sought help in many different ways.

Thus the arts of divination have flourished down through the ages. People try everything from the visiting gypsy fortune teller through palmistry, numerology, astrology, and *I Ching* (the Chinese *Book of the Changes*), to medium-consulting and various experiments with ESP. Although there is much error, and occasionally downright fraud, in each of these "arts," it is also true that many individuals are helped by the information they receive in this offbeat manner. When I began to study the occult sciences, I was fascinated by the sound advice to be gained from the *I Ching,* but I was far from the first to reach this conclusion. The great psychiatrist, Dr. Carl G. Jung, wrote the introduction to an English translation. This introduction included the interesting remark that if the book were a human being, Dr. Jung would have to judge it quite sane on the basis of its responses to questions he put to it about its introduction to the English-speaking peoples.

There may be much of value to you in one of these occult arts, especially in helping you decide what you can change at any given point in time. Of course there are other ways, including prayer and meditation, common horse sense, and even spirit guidance. We will explore many of these at appropriate places as we unfold our basic plan to help you improve all areas of your life. The important thing to remember is to use your PCP to change what can be changed *today*—and don't waste it on fruitless endeavors.

The secret of success is to formulate an over-all plan for your life. Then set attainable goals for each short run period, and parlay them into a lifetime of glorious achievement.

A man dropped out of law school because of a family financial crisis. He worked for fifteen years as a construction laborer, often bemoaning his fate. He was introduced to the principles of PCP by a friend. It took careful planning and dedication to use PCP to provide the time and money, but in just four short years he passed his bar examination and embarked on his long-delayed law career. His success as a labor specialist was almost immediate because of his years of construction experience. With PCP he was able to turn the years of apparent defeat into the raw material of extraordinary success. And *your* PCP can do the same or much more for you!

The special importance of relaxed awareness

In my last book, *Helping Yourself with ESP*,[1] I devoted pages and pages to the basic idea of *paying attention* to the inspiration and psychic impressions that let us know when our timing is right, and lead us on from success to glorious accomplishment. We called the concept *relaxed awareness* because that most perfectly describes it. If you're all tensed up and full of anxiety, the best idea in the world could walk up and slap you in the face, and you wouldn't notice the least bit of its

---

[1] Al G. Manning, *Helping Yourself with E.S.P.* (West Nyack: Parker Publishing Company, Inc., 1966).

potential. I won't belabor the point here, but I strongly suggest that you hold the idea of *relaxed awareness* close by as you go on with our self-help program. In that way you will help us give you the most for your efforts.

The special relationship between relaxed awareness and timing is virtually self-evident. How can your timing be good if your awareness is unable to pick up the little signals from the deeper parts of you? And it's that old bugaboo anxiety (or shall we call it eagerness?) that robs us of inner awareness more easily than anything else. A few years ago, I let eagerness get the momentary upper hand over my own relaxed awareness and the result set back the progress of my "pet" spiritual project by something over a year.

We have been involved since late 1959 in a combination research and public service project involving the practical applications of a "something" that can be most easily understood as *living psychic light.* Shortly after the publication of my first book, *The Miraculous Laws of Universal Dynamics,*[2] we naturally allowed a small group of interested people to petition a national organization for a church charter with the understanding that my continuing research program could be handled better as a department of the church. Because I was also deeply involved in business with work for a contractor of the Jet Propulsion Laboratory of the California Institute of Technology, it seemed proper to take our organizational pattern from them, and let the research group stand in the same relationship to the church as J. P. L. does to C. I. T. Thus far we were doing fine, but then the eagerness crept in, and in the rush to get things airborne we picked an utterly ridiculous name for the research group.

There's more to a name than meets the eye. As time moved

---

[2] Al G. Manning, *The Miraculous Laws of Universal Dynamics* (Englewood Cliffs: Prentice-Hall, Inc., 1964).

along, I was more and more embarrassed by the silly choice of the name—particularly as the response from really thinking people suffered seriously. We finally straightened it out by a name change, but I feel that it's an excellent object lesson to us all. Both names carry the idea that had been seeking expression, but the eagerness effectively blocked the proper expression when we needed it the most. Compare the old name, *Spiritual Jet Propulsion Foundation* (I still shudder), with the simplicity and dignity of the same idea allowed to properly express itself as *ESP Laboratory*. I trust that this little confession will help you remember to maintain your own relaxed awareness until the inspiration you reach out for has time to fully express itself. In other words, don't rush off half cocked like I did!

One of my good students reported success in overcoming her eagerness and holding firm for the full working of the help that is always waiting for you:

"Would you believe! This morning before I went down to sign the lease agreement "we" (the PCP guiding force and I) had a little talk. I asked for guidance and more awareness since I was going to ask her (the owner) for a change in the lease— to a 1 year/1 year option instead of 3 years. So I asked for the most persuasive energy in the business to go along with me to this meeting. Guess what! The owner readily agreed to all my proposals. . . . *and* she gave me the rent at $120 a month instead of the $125, $130 and $135 options she was asking before. How about that? And she agreed to pay for changing the door locks. (That's a big thing. As I said, it's an estate involvement where they don't want to spend two cents.) Yippee!"

This may seem like a small thing, but as we pile up many small successes by using our awareness coupled with timing, we soon find a whole life changed to the basic pattern of success. *It will work for you—every time you pay attention to it!*

Points to Remember from This Chapter

1. Your success will come as a result of careful planning and application of PCP.

2. Push the PCP firing button only after a detailed countdown.

3. The countdown should double check the proper adjustment of your desire as well as verify that you *really want* what you are seeking.

4. Forget about scientific repeatability. Just use your PCP whenever you need it.

5. Timing is of paramount importance. Use your PCP energy to change the things that can be changed *today*—don't waste it on fruitless endeavors.

6. You can change any condition in your life, if your timing is right.

7. Relaxed awareness is your key to using the full force of your PCP.

how to

Organize a Plan to
Make PCP Work for You

In any undertaking, *progress can be sustained only by effective work under a carefully organized plan.* Oh yes, there are some successes that happen by accident, but the batting average of organization is a hundred times better than that of accident. It's only prudence to play the percentages and stick to good organization.

Examples of careful planning

The great aerospace industry, in association with our National Aeronautics and Space Administration, provides an excellent series of examples of the value of careful planning. This industry is facing and solving problems which men didn't even dream existed a few years ago. Some of the results are nearly incredible. For instance, the spectacular success of one Mariner flyby mission to Mars was described as the equivalent in reliability to your home color television set's operating continuously for over five hundred years without any maintenance.

Consider the complexity of the program to land the first Americans on the moon. Literally thousands of people were involved over a period of many years, doing many seemingly trivial and unimportant tasks. But an over-all plan, implemented by a series of sub-plans, tied all the tiny bits of individual effort into the feats of glory that were the Mercury shots which paved the way for Gemini, and finally the Apollo missions themselves.

The goals you set for yourself may not be as spectacular as landing a man on the moon, but they will be much more important to you personally. Let's take a closer look at the NASA formula for success. Think of the task itself, back near the beginning. It was necessary to develop a whole new series of technologies to begin the approach. As in the case of your own advancement, many problems must be solved before anything like measurable success begins to show. NASA researched such divergent areas as rocket propulsion, equipment performance in a vacuum, navigation and control of spacecraft, human reaction to weightlessness and confinement in a small space for many days, re-entry heat dissipation, protection of personnel and equipment from radiation, and hundreds of others. But all this effort was planned and coordinated—it didn't just happen. It works like this: the top level planning group defines the over-all mission and breaks it down into a series of sub-missions which can be operated in parallel and series to wind up together in the complete package. Then each sub-mission is broken down into major tasks, the major tasks into sub-tasks and sub-sub-tasks, until finally the tiny tasks are comprehensible to small groups of engineers and technicians at the working level. Only then can the actual work be started.

To apply this success formula to your own life, the obvious first step is to set the over-all goal, to define the major mission. This may be harder than it first seems. What do you want to do with your life? How do you want to be remembered after you have passed on? Why did you come to this earth life in the first place? Most of us are not yet prepared to give our final answers to questions like these, so let's defer them to the second half of this book. For now we will concern ourselves with simpler goals that we can grasp easily in our minds. How about a nice general goal of steady improvement in all areas of life? This will prepare us to cope with the deeper philosophical problems from a position of lessened pressure from our daily problems. And it gives us a set of coordinates from which to set up an excellent group of sub-goals like improvement of our finances, peace of mind, health, love life, circle of friends, effectiveness, and accomplishments. Of course we will have to plan in much greater detail than a mere set of general goals. And again we will find our help in a look at the example of the aerospace industry.

The PERT concept

The first Polaris missile was being developed for the Navy Special Projects Office. As a means of balancing time, cost, and performance, the PERT concept was evolved. Pert is a coined word, taken from the first letter of each word of its longer title, Program Evaluation and Review Technique. The system was so successful it spread quickly throughout the industry and became the cornerstone of planning for NASA projects as well as major weapons systems.

Some form of PERT is being used to control and manage every major scientific project financed by the Department of Defense or NASA, but it has also spread out into non-governmental projects. Its enthusiastic proponents have adapted PERT for various hobby-type projects. It has even been used in theater productions of the Pasadena Playhouse. But exactly what is PERT? Basically it is a master plan which shows the interrelationships of every tiny event that must occur in order to reach your goal on schedule. Because it is concerned with their interrelationships, it points out the areas where there is room for reshuffling and flexibility as well as the areas which fall along the "critical path" or area whose schedule slippage will result in the whole project being late by like amounts of time.

Let's illustrate PERT with a simple task like preparing a dinner to be ready at six o'clock. The over-all goal is dinner on schedule, but immediately we are concerned with the sub-goals or specific sequence of events which must take place before the end result is accomplished. Some of these tasks can be done in parallel, but others cannot be started until a prior task has been completed. For instance, you could not begin to cook the potatoes until they were first brought from the grocery store and/or removed from their storage place. We begin by listing the steps one might take in preparing the meal for six o'clock delivery.

To make the process easily understandable, we will greatly oversimplify the tasks, and assume a simple menu of marinated steak, French fried potatoes, and green salad. We will also assume that all necessary ingredients are available in the kitchen so that no procurement activities are necessary. We can therefore make the following list of events:

1. Prepare marinade.
2. Marinate steak.
3. Preheat broiler.
4. Start cooking steak.
5. Turn steak.
6. Steak ready to serve.
7. Peel and slice potatoes.
8. Preheat cooking fat.
9. Start cooking potatoes.
10. Potatoes ready to serve.
11. Cut salad ingredients.

12. Dress salad.
13. Salad ready.
14. Set table.
15. Serve dinner.
16. Dinner served.

You will note that some of these events involve actions while others involve waiting for something to happen. In a real PERT problem, minimum times will be assigned for the successful accomplishment of each task-event. Those events which cannot start until a previous task has been completed will be properly coded. Then all the information is fed into a computer, digested, and the data for a complete PERT Chart printed out. We purposely kept our example simple enough to grasp without the assistance of a computer, but the logic involved is essentially the same. Since we want the whole group of events to culminate simultaneously into a happy dinner, the simplest approach is to start with the time we expect to serve, and work backwards to determine the exact time we must begin preparations. Then we can draw the "critical path" of events we must keep on schedule if we are to meet our deadline.

Figure 1 shows the chart we would prepare from the list of events above. Notice that actions are denoted by circles with elapsed time of the action written on the solid line connecting with the next event. Events of a waiting nature are shown by squares with dotted lines connecting with the next event.

Again the elapsed time is shown along the line. In this illustration, the critical path of 80 minutes is shown by the heavy black line which follows the critical events. In this case it can be seen to flow along the preparation of the steak, then in parallel through the cooking of both the steak and potatoes to the serving of the completed meal. We see that we have plenty of leeway in the time of setting the table and preparing the

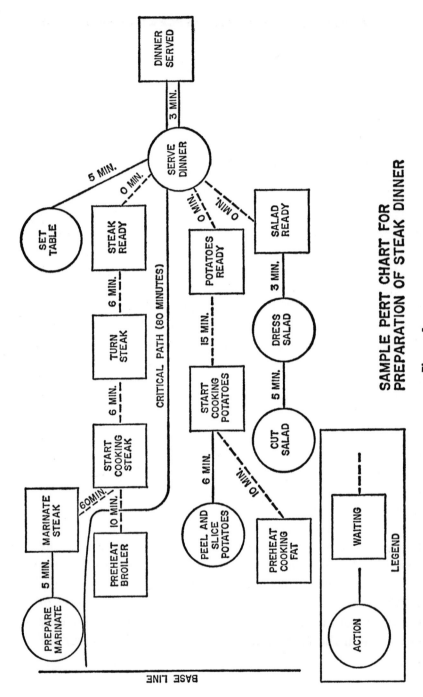

SAMPLE PERT CHART FOR
PREPARATION OF STEAK DINNER

Figure 1.

salad, and things don't really get very busy until about the last 30 minutes. Therefore we have some time after starting the project which we can safely devote to other projects, just so long as we monitor our position on the chart and keep on schedule along the critical path.

This may seem like a whole lot of nonsense as applied to a "simple" thing like cooking an easy dinner, but it is similar to the process any good cook goes through mentally to get a meal to the table hot and on time. However our purpose isn't to improve your culinary skill! Rather we are presenting an organized approach to improving your whole life. Whether you are considering a major long-term goal, or a simple short-term thing like getting dinner, it can be better understood and scheduled by applying simplified PERT logic. This is the way to come up with a master plan which pinpoints the areas of flexibility and the *critical path* that must be kept on schedule. Then when life gets overly busy or tough, you know in advance what sub-projects you can temporarily shelve, and which ones you must push with all your available effort.

Where major long-term goals (like finding, wooing, and marrying your perfect mate) are involved, you may not see all the way to the end of the sequence, but you *can* PERT the obvious steps which will lead you closer to ultimate achievement. There isn't enough time in the day to PERT each task in detail to the end of your lifetime, but a little judgment will show you what needs intricate planning and what may be safely slipped for the time being. A crude master PERT Chart for your life's ultimate goals as you now view them would be very useful—thus you will know what projects lie along the critical path and require your concentrated effort, and consequently what other projects may be handled on a hobby or leisure basis. You can apply PERT as a practical tool to guide you to the achievement of any goal you choose to set for yourself.

How to master it now and multiply it into a successful future

Most people float like toothpicks on the river of life, drifting about and changing direction with every little shift of wind or current. When you ask someone where he is going you may get an answer like, "The poorhouse," "The grave," "Straight to hell," or just plain "Crazy." And that's *all* the thought normally given to the subject! If you press a man like that, he may speculate with you for a while, but he will quickly develop a burning desire to escape to the nearest bar, bowling alley, or golf course. It would be nice to help him, but he instinctively refuses it.

We might bemoan the state of the collective consciousness that permits such a slothlike intellectual condition, but that would accomplish nothing. Instead, take heart that you can apply a little organization to your own life and quickly outdistance the masses. And in the process you will be doing the most you can to awaken the sleeping mass mind. Anyone who honestly helps himself helps all mankind at the same time. The first requirement is to formulate a set of goals. Decide what you want to achieve financially, intellectually, socially, and spiritually. Long-term goals are of special value to us. They give us a solid framework within which to construct practical short-term goals, and they are excellent for providing encouragement when we contemplate them in our quiet moments.

But the key element of success is steady striving to meet realistic short-term goals, and the immediate replacement of accomplished tasks with new ones. Resting on your laurels will never accomplish anything but a middle age spread! However it is equally important that we waste no PCP energy in moaning over what might have been, or what can't be reached in the short term. A minor divergence for a peek at Raja Yoga will help us here. The lesson of Raja Yoga is to learn concentration. Do each task for its own sake and to the best of your ability. If you continually look ahead to what you hope to be doing a few hours or minutes from now, you are not doing justice to *this moment*. Planning is important, but precise execution of each step is the only way to accomplishment.

We must strive to continually improve our judgment and timing. There is a time for planning and PERT Charts, a time for enthusiastic execution of your plans, and a time for re-evaluation and adjustment of your course of action to accommodate unforeseen developments.

Adjust your short-term goals as the project develops

Again we can learn much from NASA. We occasionally witness the postponement of a major space shot because of unfavorable weather. It seems incongruous that a mission which will circle the earth thirty or more times, or head for a distant planet, must wait for a little rain squall to pass over the launch area. But prudence wins out over face-saving, and the mission is postponed until its chances of success are maximum.

This is an example of the flexibility of planning which directs itself to maximum probability of success with the minimum risk of personnel and equipment. Flexibility in planning means your willingness to bend when you are confronted with situations beyond your immediate control. Consider also the example of the reed which bends with the wind—if it were rigid, it would be broken off like the dead limb of a tree.

A young man had been in the accounting department of a medium size corporation for several years. He dreamed of becoming controller, and eventually treasurer, of this growing enterprise. There had been no advancement for three years when, quite unexpectedly, he was offered the chance to fill a vacancy in the marketing department. His first reaction was to refuse because this seemed to lead away from his chosen goal. But he understood the need for flexibility, so he swallowed hard and accepted the challenge. As matters turned out, he never did become controller of his company, but he did become a highly successful Vice President for Marketing.

We must be sure to understand that *flexibility is not lack of purpose.* It is the finely-tempered judgment that knows when to stop hitting your head against a brick wall. Why wait thirty years to become a controller when you have the latent talent and aptitude to become a marketing vice president in less than five? And how shall you know if you have necessary ability? Be guided by the opportunities as they come to you. No intelligent executive will offer a position to a man he doesn't think can fill it. Shouldn't that be good enough for you also? Keep moving in the general direction of success, but adjust your short-term goals to bend around the obstacles and grab the opportunities as life brings them your way.

Points to Remember from This Chapter

1. Progress is the result of effective work under a carefully organized plan.

2. The PERT concept is an excellent tool for both short- and long-term planning.

3. Use PERT to make your *now* most effective.

4. Maintain a positive flexibility as you strive, but never lose sight of the ultimate goal.

how to

Promote Coordination Between Your Various PCP Plans

We studied PERT in the last chapter to learn how to schedule and monitor our short-term accomplishments. Now we will work on a broader chart. It's time to lay out the master plan for evolution of your life as a whole. Keep in mind that your personal chart should be considerably more specific than the sample we will create here. You know the special areas of your personality and life conditions that need the most careful attention. These should be placed in the key positions.

How to construct your personal Master Plan

Instead of listing specific events as we did in preparing our PERT Chart, we will list the areas of your life that are to be changed. We will need to develop as much understanding of their interrelationships as possible. The simplest way to begin is by listing the areas of our concern:

1. Enthusiasm and zest for life
2. Flow of money, and financial well being

3. Peace of mind
4. Health and vitality
5. Application of the self to each activity
6. Circle of friends
7. Personal popularity
8. Meaning to life
9. Effectiveness in all undertakings
10. Freedom from uncomfortable people and conditions
11. Marital bliss
12. Intuition and extra-sensory-perception
13. Accomplishment
14. Expression
15. Fulfillment
16. Personal relationship to God

Next we translate the list into a *representative Master Plan for improving your life*. Figure 2 is the Master Plan developed from the sixteen areas listed above. Look for the special value of using the chart form to develop the closest interrelationships.

A few moments spent in contemplation of the chart will reveal that an improvement in just one box of your chart will work to the benefit and improvement of all the others. Similarly, one very bad box may drag the whole superstructure down to its level. This points up the need for a period of introspection. Try to list your general areas in order from the weakest to the strongest.

Somebody will say it is altogether impossible to rank all sixteen areas in the exact order of their progressive strength. And he is undoubtedly right. We don't have to be nitpickers about this thing. A broad brush ranking will do nicely. It's also true that the order of this ranking will change continually as we bring our PCP powers to bear on one after the other.

The reason for this exercise is to decide which area of your life needs attention first. It's still a basic limitation of the human attention span that it cannot embrace more than one or

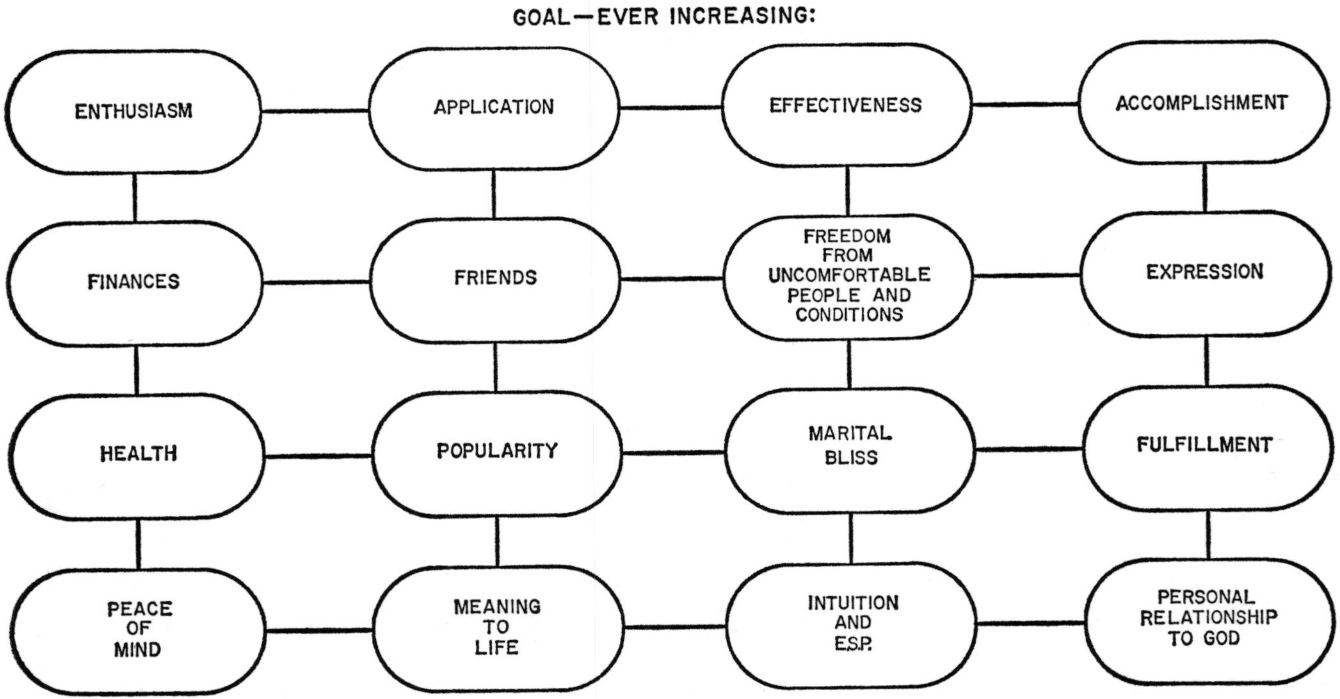

GOAL—EVER INCREASING:

ENTHUSIASM	APPLICATION	EFFECTIVENESS	ACCOMPLISHMENT
FINANCES	FRIENDS	FREEDOM FROM UNCOMFORTABLE PEOPLE AND CONDITIONS	EXPRESSION
HEALTH	POPULARITY	MARITAL BLISS	FULFILLMENT
PEACE OF MIND	MEANING TO LIFE	INTUITION AND E.S.P.	PERSONAL RELATIONSHIP TO GOD

REPRESENTATIVE MASTER PLAN
FOR IMPROVING YOUR LIFE

Figure 2.

two things at a time. The deep concentration needed to effectively use PCP will limit us to just one area at a time. However, some will find that they can run more than one project in parallel. Let's look at a few examples of how others have worked these laws to attain really excellent results.

How to let an increasing flow of money buy you more peace of mind and more time for spiritual study and growth

A young widow with three children decided that money was her most limiting factor. She applied all her psychic attention to learning the true Cosmic laws of supply—she corrected her negative attitude toward money, then started to apply Psycho-Cosmic Power to increase her income. Within three weeks her attitude had materially changed. She was brighter and better looking. When she was offered a new job at $30 per week more than she had been making, she accepted gratefully. She was amazed to find the new set of working conditions less demanding than her old job. Thus she had more energy and time left for spiritual study and meditation.

Following the over-all plan of her master chart, she let the increased flow of money buy her more peace of mind, and so more opportunity for spiritual growth. The new-found happiness and growth showed in her outward appearance and personality more and more each day. Within three months she attracted a man of similar interests who was quite smitten with her newly-acquired radiance. Time proved they were ideally suited for each other. They were married and used their PCP as a team to bring more and more good into their lives. He is now a very successful executive, and she is an ecstatically happy housewife. Both are growing in spirit steadily, and you could honestly apply the fairy tale ending here—"and they lived happily ever after."

This can be the story of your own life if you will apply the lessons set forth in the following chapters. Psycho-Cosmic Power is the sleeping giant, awaiting only the command to serve you. Be careful that you command its use only for the *good* of yourself and others.

**How to let increased health and vitality
improve your alertness and ability to
concentrate**

A freshman was on the verge of flunking out of college. Nervous tension kept his stomach upset and full of gas, and he seemed to have a headache almost constantly. While seeking about for help, he encountered the PCP idea. He immediately began to apply PCP to his health condition. He was led to understand that his nervous tension was caused by taking himself and all of life too seriously. Next came the difficult task of transforming his intellectual acceptance of the idea into a feeling-reaction pattern of relaxed living.

This is not a story of immediate smashing success. But the student did manage enough change to make it through his freshman year with a C average and only about half the physical problems of the peak of his troubles. During his sophomore year he noticed that a chain reaction was beginning to work in his favor. Each bit of progress toward relieving his physical symptoms helped to lessen his nervous tension. And as he got rid of the tension, the physical symptoms naturally subsided. A big side benefit was his increasing ability to concentrate on his studies. And again, as his grades improved, his nervous tension further subsided.

The chain reaction of good continued as he enthusiastically applied himself to the constructive use of PCP. By his junior year he was chalking up a straight B average, and he began to notice a new side benefit. His growing ability to concentrate during his spiritual meditation periods lead him to an entirely new relationship to God. He regularly experienced what Freud calls the "oceanic feeling" during his meditations, and this seemed to expand his consciousness and add to his over-all grasp of life's deeper meaning. He has taken his place as one of society's most effective citizens, and continues his growth by daily application of Psycho-Cosmic Power.

You can use PCP to heal any physical condition, including the so-called "incurable" diseases. The power is infinite! Its only limitation is in the mind of the person using it. A little later we will go into detail on just how you can heal yourself and your loved ones. You are entitled to live a healthy, prosperous, exciting life. Start claiming it now!

Let enthusiasm add a new dimension to your popularity

On her eighteenth birthday, Bonnie received a book, *The Edinburgh Lectures on Mental Science,* by Thomas Troward.[1] It captured her fancy, and she began to apply its basic teachings with childlike enthusiasm. She knew she had a rather drab personality which one might call the wallflower type. She asserted that "Infinite Spirit" was changing her personality completely, replacing all shyness and negativity with boundless enthusiasm and energy.

Bonnie promised herself that every encounter with another person would be treated as an opportunity to express the joy and enthusiasm of infinite life. Ten minutes after she made this promise her telephone rang. It was an unexpected invitation to a party from a boy she knew only casually. She accepted graciously, and mentally acknowledged this as her challenge to

---

[1] Thomas Troward, *The Edinburgh Lectures on Mental Science* (London: Fowler & Company, 1956).

prove she could be a channel of divine enthusiasm. She "let the Infinite Spirit manifest itself through her" at the party and had more fun than at any time she could remember. She honestly became the life of that party, and went on to attain a popularity and zest for life beyond anything she had dreamed possible.

Enthusiasm is pure PCP. Let these ideas begin to express as enthusiasm in your life. It will carry you to heights of achievement and happiness past the limits of imagination.

How to program your subconscious to work with PCP all the time

One night my wife suffered for several hours with some "normal" female pains. She told me about it the next morning, laughing at herself. "When I finally remembered to ask that the pain be removed, it was gone in less than three minutes!" she chuckled. "But I suffered needlessly for a long time before I had sense enough to ask for help."

The secret of true success is the habit of using PCP constantly. As you put PCP uppermost in your mind, you will derive the most benefit. The normal pressures of daily living tend to crowd out abstract thoughts of this nature. It is of utmost importance to develop habit patterns of turning back to PCP at every spare moment, and every critical moment as well. We spend many hours of each day performing routine tasks that can be handled while the mind is occupied with controlling and directing PCP. For instance:

1. The shower or bath, and time spent shaving (or while you ladies are putting on your makeup) is excellent for amplifying your PCP by the use of properly constructed affirmations, and the direction of your thoughts to things like health, power and accomplishment.

2. Difficult meetings, or encounters with difficult people, provide excellent opportunities to practice the use of PCP. Get your ideas across and maintain such tranquility within yourself that it sets the tone of the whole meeting.
3. The drive to and from work, or any other driving time, is excellent for focusing your PCP energy on special problems.

The busier you are, the more important it is to use your PCP constantly. As you make PCP a habit, you will find it going ahead of you to make your path easy and your way straight.

How to use PCP to refine your Master Plan

This chapter's opening discussion concerned making a Master Plan for improving your life. Let's assume you have made the first draft of your plan, and set out to improve it. The more nearly the plan fits your special personality and aptitudes, the more immediately successful you will become.

The best way to improve a plan is to treat it like any other PCP project. First refresh your contact with the PCP frequency, then express your desire in compatible terms. Here you carefully review each item listed on your chart to be sure it is stated in the most positive terms. Here we must maintain a fine balance between being exactingly specific and generalizing where necessary to eliminate lurking negativity. The representative Master Plan for improving your life (Figure 2) might be refined to specifics for a college student majoring in marketing. This is illustrated in Figure 3. Study this example and work to refine your own plan along these lines.

But let's keep our perspective. Your Master Plan is useful only if you implement it with short term goals. These are the tasks and subtasks which are completely specific in nature and lend themselves to the PERT Technique discussed in Chapter

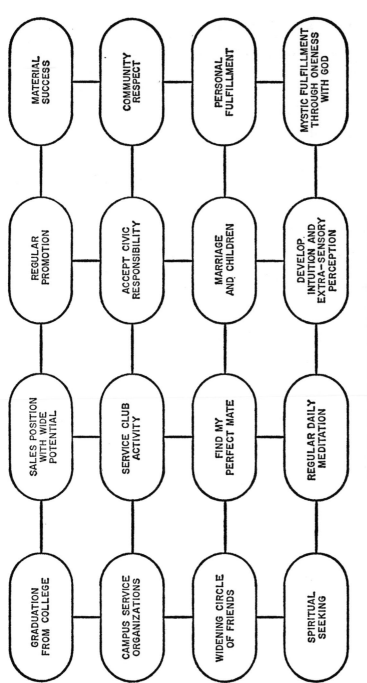

MODEL PLAN FOR IMPROVING A LIFE

Figure 3.

3. We close this section with a thought intended to put planning in its right relationship to life.

People who achieve their short-term goals go on from success to success, and they are far better off than those who ignore the small while idly dreaming of greatness.

Points to Remember from This Chapter

1. Construct a Master Plan for the improvement of your life.

2. Study the interrelatedness of the important areas of your life and try to list them in order from the weakest to the strongest.

3. Apply your PCP to the weakest area and let its improvement reflect progress to all the other areas.

4. Program your subconscious to use PCP all the time.

5. Regularly use PCP to refine and improve your Master Plan.

6. Keep your perspective. Never forget that success is the result of achieving short-term goals.

how to
Use PCP to Attract
More Money and Lead
the Abundant Life

Let's get back to the area of the immediately practical, and turn our attention to the age-old problem of money. Money is a fascinating commodity because it means so many different things to different people. To one it means the hope of a square meal or a decent pair of shoes, to another it may mean the way to finance Saturday night's date, others look at it as security, and still others as power. Doesn't it mean a little of each to you? What does it take to attract money?

Hard work isn't always the answer

More than one good management consultant has this motto on his desk: *Don't confuse effort with results!* It's obvious that an executive who makes $100,000 a year doesn't work four times as hard or put in four times the hours of a $25,000 a year man. Yet he commands the difference in the executive market place. Why?

An acquaintance of mine bought corporate stock at 6½ and

told a friend he thought it was a good investment opportunity. Almost immediately, the stock started to drop. The friend purchased a larger block of the same stock at 3%. By the time the stock had climbed back to 4½, the first man felt impelled to sell and take his loss. The second man held on a little longer and then sold his at 9½. Thus the second man made a nice profit on the advice of a man who lost money in the same investment. Why?

By hard physical labor a man can earn a reasonably comfortable four-digit income. But the five- and six-figure plums are always held by people who have learned a few extra things about the art of making money.

What is the secret of financial success? Our first clue lies back on the management consultant's desk. *Don't confuse effort with results!* The next clue can be found in your attitude toward money. This is so important we might call it your launch pad for financial success.

How to build your launch pad for financial success

In ancient times man's symbols of wealth were readily recognizable. One's worldly means took the form of sheep, cattle, oxen, and the like. These were the living evidence of continued sustenance, freedom from famine, and as much security as offered by the times.

As civilization became more complex, man found it necessary to substitute symbols for more cumbersome tangible commodities. Thus was born the concept of a medium of exchange. The symbols used sometimes had no intrinsic value, such as shells or leaves. And at other times there was an underlying value like the metal in gold or silver coins. Later the abstract concept of the bank balance came along and eliminated all but the smaller movements of even the symbols of wealth. But somehow, the more abstract the medium of exchange, the more people seem to get an idea that there is something almost immoral about it.

It is extremely important that you get your ideas about money clarified and put in the most positive light. Let's be sure we understand exactly what it is. *Money is simply a symbol of sustenance,* and as such it is the evidence of nature's abundance—God's *givingness.* Wherever there is life we find nature carefully providing for its nourishment and propagation. The Great Way-Shower explained this beautifully: *Behold the fowls of the air: for they sow not, neither do they reap, nor gather into barns; yet your Heavenly Father feedeth them. Are ye not much better than they? . . . Consider the lilies of the fields, how they grow; they toil not, neither do they spin: and yet I say unto you, that even Solomon in all his glory was not arrayed like one of these. Wherefore, if God so clothe the grass of the field, which today is, and tomorrow is cast into the oven, shall he not much more clothe you . . . ?* (Matthew 5.)

Remember that money is simply a symbol of God's wonderful givingness. The sunshine and rain are given freely to all; they fall alike upon the just and the unjust. The Infinite Opulence is likewise offered to all by a generous and loving God. But it is up to you to construct a vessel to collect it! It can be compared to a great rushing stream. You can carry a small cup and drink as you need it, or you may carry home a large bucketful. The limitation is not in the supply, but merely in your container and your capacity to carry it home.

We can never say enough about the value of proper attitude. Because money is so very responsive to mental laws, your attitude toward money is a basic key to financial success. In *The Miraculous Laws of Universal Dynamics,* I set forth the *law of attraction and repulsion.* Let's quote it here to show exactly how your mental-emotional patterns control the flow of money in your life:

That which you give, or would willingly give, you attract; and that which you withhold, or strongly desire to withhold, you repel.

Properly grounded in the context of this natural law, your attitude and approach toward the broad subject of money is your launching pad to financial success. Take care to build one strong enough to facilitate your "liftoff." You must always think and speak well of money. Understand that the Universal Power which we have called the PCP principle, desires to express through you as ever growing abundance. In plain language: *God's Will for you is always ever-increasing abundance!*

Learn to think like a person having an abundance of money. This means that you will naturally appreciate the many positive values of modern business. Your every conversation about the business world will be positive and constructive in nature. You won't gloss over the weaknesses of our capitalistic economy, but your desire will be to strengthen and improve it—you will certainly *never* complain about it! In the same way, you will rejoice in the wealth of others! Since you have infinite abundance, you have no reason to be envious of another's wealth or suspicious of the means of its accumulation. You will become a real team player, ever working, talking, and acting for the good of all. This is a perfect application of the law of attraction and repulsion. Your desire and work for the good of all must attract the most good to you also.

As a person of means, you will feel no urge to cheat, grasp, or horde. It is your earnest intention to give value for value at all times, lest you negatively operate that same law of attraction and repulsion. You will regularly pay your debts, and meet each financial obligation promptly. All this is part of thinking and acting as a person of opulence. The stronger you build this launching pad, the more certain your chances of blasting off into a new atmosphere of riches and abundance.

As you make these ideas part of your very being, you begin

setting the great PCP forces into operation. And it must manifest your abundance! Accept it, and *enjoy* the whole idea of money as a Cosmic Force for Good.

**Now tune your consciousness to the
PCP money broadcast**

You will regularly get the best results if you renew your contact with the Psycho-Cosmic Power before each specific use. There are two reasons for this. First, your daily routine tends to lull you into forgetfulness of the wonderful power you are tapping, thus your contact may fade perceptibly. You must bring the power to its greatest strength in you, each time you expect to use it effectively.

The second reason is perhaps more important. We may compare your PCP receiving apparatus to a radio or television set. During the routine of your daily existence, you leave the set tuned to nice, soothing background music because this enhances your enjoyment and efficiency. But there are also times when you want to use your "set" to pick up a special news broadcast or your favorite religious program. This requires that you change the tuning to a preselected frequency.

Similarly, as you sit in your quiet place, carefully choose the specific purpose of the attunement you seek. In other words, decide what new station you want to receive. In this chapter, your purpose is to tune in on the *material abundance frequency* on your PCP dial. Announce the purpose to your own consciousness, then begin to slowly intone the mystic mantra, *Om mane padme hum.* As you repeat the mantra, mentally claim that you are tuning to the abundance frequency, and *feel* the growing power of your perfect PCP attunement.

Feel, as a fact, the great waves of PCP energy flowing into your being. Then spend a few minutes relaxing in the warm inner glow of it. It is only from this position of attunement that you can effectively operate the next step, the expression of your financial desires in terms of PCP.

Express your financial desires in terms of PCP

Here the work of building your launching pad begins to pay off. The basic ideas which mould your desires and make them compatible with the PCP principle have already been made part of your being. You already understand that the great universal law is growth and expansion, and that money is merely a symbol of sustenance. Now we'll look just a little farther.

The Hindu concept of *prana* will help us to understand. *Prana* is the *life-giving substance.* It is the essence of physical energy and the power of growth and regeneration. *Prana* comes to us from the sun along with the scientifically known substances of sunlight. It permeates the atmosphere and is taken into our bodies as part of the normal breathing process. This is one good reason for the breathing exercises which stress rhythmic breath retention. It aids the body's assimilation of *prana* and distribution of the life giving force to the areas needing revitalization. But what does all this have to do with money? Simply that, to the Hindu, *money is the material expression of prana.*

The concept of *prana* is similar and compatible with the Christian idea of the Holy Breath. The next step is to feel the Holy Breath of Prosperity breathing new life and vigor into all of your financial affairs. This is the soundest possible basis of expressing your financial desires in terms of PCP. Your desire should be simply that the Holy Breath of Prosperity fill your body and financial affairs with success and wonderful growth. If you wish to be more specific and claim the Holy Prana for a special situation or project, that's all right. But first make sure that the purpose and means of manifestation of the project are themselves in harmony with the PCP principles.

Continue mentally claiming the Holy Breath of the PCP principle as you softly repeat the mystic mantra, and *feel* your own desire being passed over to become the desire of the Cosmic Itself. When you have passed your desire over to the Cosmic, you are certain of success. Who or what could stand against all the power of the universe?

Don't hesitate to push the PCP "start" button!

The great value of the countdown is to minimize the number of failures, and thus minimize your disappointments and frustrations. Unfamiliarity with equipment and operating procedures is a fertile breeding ground for mistakes. I had this brought home to me most vividly while learning to operate a small data-processing installation. Now of course, it seems quite simple, but for the first few days it seemed that all I could get the contraptions to do was to get them into confused patterns, and light up the "tilt" bulb. Even when all the setups and programs were carefully made and integrated, little things kept getting in the way. One machine not in the start position, or the card reader on manual instead of automatic, or the intercoupled keypunch out of phase with the rest of the system—it all seemed calculated to transform a simple electro-mechanical operation into a maze of frustration and wasted effort. But a few days of familiarity dissolved all the problems in the joy of accomplishment.

The timing angle of the countdown is probably the hardest to get your teeth into at first. Practice will bring the development of your own techniques, and a natural sense of timing will grow within you. Since this timing could hardly be wrong in the seeking of broad financial growth, we will proceed with the balance of our countdown.

Are you sure you have refined your desires until they are completely compatible with the PCP principles? Are you in tune with the PCP energy so that you feel it flowing freely throughout your being? Do you think and act like a person of opulence? Have you passed your desire over to the cosmic?

When you can give an unqualified *yes* to each countdown question, you are ready. Mentally push the firing button and say aloud, "I now launch my PCP rocket and release this desire for financial growth and abundance into the loving care of the cosmic. The infinite Psycho-Cosmic Power is moving, and it cannot fail to be manifest!" Then let go completely and visualize your desire-rocket soaring up into the reaches of PCP space to accomplish its wonderful mission.

Like any other space age project, *all PCP shots should be monitored.* Your first thought as you awaken each morning should be that your PCP rocket is on course and on schedule. Greet the new day with heartfelt thanks for the continued success of the mission. Then end each day with a thought of thanksgiving for your ever-increasing prosperity which is now the law of the universe. Go through each day's routine full of the happy expectancy of new opportunities for the advancement of your career and the enhancement of your over-all financial position. This brings us to the final step in financial unfoldment.

Let PCP bring you an ever-growing divine surplus

The key word in this step is *LET*. You have stirred up and organized all the power of the universe to work for your financial well being. But even so vast a force as the infinite PCP energy can't make you accept and use its help if you are *too tense or insensitive to notice it.*

Permit me to use an example of tangible help which took place while I was writing this book. We have a long-term, spirit-psychic research program underway that involves working to help people who contact us through the mail. I quote from a letter, typical of many:

> . . . I need your prayer therapy. My husband has just lost his job because of mental illness. He is 58 years old. I am 52 and have never worked outside my home. Anyway there is no work to get where we live. I don't know what to do. Please help me. I do believe in God and believe He answers prayer.

Our response included brief instructions on how to tune in on the PCP energy we direct to those we seek to help. I quote the balance of our letter:

> When we took your letter into our prayer period, we were shown a small purple cross (purple is the symbol of spiritual power) with a shaft coming out in front of it. There seemed to be a profusion of gold coins flowing down the shaft and into the room through the cross. This is a strong indication of really powerful spirit assistance.
> We continued to ask what advice Spirit might have for you. I felt a spirit hand placed on top of my head as if in blessing. You have plenty of help. Give thanks in prayer, and accept it.

Thirty-two days later we received this response:

> I wrote recently and asked for help for my husband who was laid off his job because of mental sickness. They didn't intend to ever let him work again. But now the doctor has declared him well and he is back on his regular job. Thank God!!! He has also found friends and has been going fishing, something he never did before in his life.

I write this happily, in the secure knowledge that Psycho-Cosmic Power has worked for me over and over, and it will continue to work for me as long as I cooperate. And since it is a natural phenomenon, *it must work for you as well.* Progress and happiness are yours! You have but to use these simple principles and nothing will be impossible to you.

Follow the urges your PCP will regularly send you. Apply them with a touch of common sense and a healthy dash of enthusiasm. Then enjoy watching your life unfold with wealth and riches. Nature is lavish and abundant with those who follow its laws. Expect not mere improvement in the flow of necessities, but an ever-growing divine surplus. Use your growing wealth wisely, but spend it ungrudgingly.

More examples of PCP powered financial blessings

I'd like to share a few more homely examples of the tangible help that has come to people who take the trouble to seek help. These are all taken from the files of our little research/service department, *ESP Laboratory:*

> I received your first membership form on February 11th. I filled it in the next day and mailed it on Monday the 13th (asking for financial help). The previous Thursday I had been interviewed for a position, but when I called the agency, the employer had not made up his mind. I felt it was the right position for me and I really wanted it, as it was a $100-a-month increase from my previous job and things have been pretty bad financially with me.
>
> The following Thursday he called and said he wanted me. I am grateful for the prayers that week, as I know it was because of them that I got the job. I started my new job on the first of March, and with the help of the prayers from the *ESP Laboratory* and with all the growth I am obtaining every day from reading *The Miraculous Laws of Universal Dynamics,* I know it is finally an answer to working at a job I will thoroughly enjoy and which will be the answer to my financial problems.

A lady from Kalamazoo wrote:

Last month I asked for help for a retiree who *had* to find an apartment for $50 tops. It had seemed impossible in this college town. I wrote Tuesday and you probably got it before Saturday. Sunday she found one for $50 in the house she had owned for nine years, so she took it without ever inspecting it. She is most happy, but stretching the balance of her social security over food, clothes and incidentals is still a tightrope job. Please keep her on for another month of prosperity treatment. And thank you Father, Al, Laboratory, and Invisible Friends above, for your successful accomplishments.

A gentleman from Ohio told us:

I wish to report that things are looking up again. I made some extra money last week for the first time in years. I still am in need, but am thankful and pray God's blessing on you and your work! The *lights* are not too clear yet, but I'll keep trying. I need the *light* for healing my vision, but I feel that it's coming. I am grateful.

And this one from a long-time friend (whom I hope to meet in the flesh one of these days) in Pennsylvania made me specially happy. She wrote just last month to say:

Oh I have so much to tell you, where to begin? First off—I have a brand new job which fell out of the blue (We are used to things coming out of the blue though, so why be surprised?). But I was, I'm new at this as you well know. And happenings do surprise and delight me. That's what is so wonderful about all this; I can mentally clap my hands and say, "It's happening to me!" and experience that thrill, that *joy*.

Remember my telling you about the C's, and blind T, and the K's? The folks I sorta "mother-henned": well the Office of Economic Opportunity in this War on Poverty Act are appointing what is known as

"Neighborhood Aides" to be placed in the area in which they reside to act as liaison workers between the various services available in the state and county and the people, and to inform the agencies of the needs of the people, and the people of the services of the agencies—people like the ones I mentioned above, blind, health, aged, etc. I've been fighting my own war on poverty for years for this kind of people, and now I'm to be paid for it. How about that!

Let me tell you how it happened. One morning my door bell rang and a very nicely dressed man stood there, a stranger. (I know most everyone in the area.) He asked, "Are you Mrs. M?"

"Yes."

"May I come in? I'm Mr. —— from Washington."

He showed me some credentials and I of course thought of my boy in the service. I said, "Is it about my son?"

And he said, "Oh no, it's about you."

So I asked him in and as I was about to have breakfast coffee I invited him to join me. Then he told me of this appointment. He explained that my neighbors had submitted my name and asked that it be kept as a surprise until I had been approved. My goodness, I was flabbergasted! And my mom and my sister were in on it—co-conspirators, the stinkers! Mom even sneaking out my birth certificate. I'm leaving early this morning to go to Temple University in Philadelphia for a fifteen-day course, and when I come back I will have my own office just one street away from my home. The folks have donated a desk and chairs, and the neighbors are painting it. They won't even let me see it. —Hey, remember me? I'm the gal that got fired last summer and you wrote these words to me—"C, *there may be a goose that will lay a golden egg, don't let some idiot spoil it for you!*" Oh, Al, what a responsibility you took on when you wrote these books, for see, *I believe everything you say*— Let me ask you this—Can I do this job? I'm a little bit scared, just a little. Will I fail the people I love? Can you take this to the altar for me?

I then had the happy task of writing her a reassuring letter, and I'd like to give you just a bit of her reply:

> My dear, your words of reassurance give me such impetus—and truly humility. I have a feeling that I am developing a sort of "mission" (not the bowl of soup, sermonette kind, but the talk it out kind). There are some incredibly dedicated persons in this program, right here in this community. There are around ten men and an equal number of women that I can count on. I wasn't aware of this—but I know now— the problem is to make people see that their decisions do make a difference; to make them responsive and responsible citizens. I want to awaken them to the fact that they are part of God's creation, and ought to benefit from all its loveliness, but also teach them that they have a job to do in maintaining it. But make no mistake, mere ideals are not what these people need, they need help to get them better housing, jobs, food, medical care, and all the rest of these services. . . . Before I was only Rachel weeping for my children, but now I have a handful of persons behind me with "guts" who are willing to say ACTION, no more promises. . . .

What can I add to this, except to say that these people are not just a "lucky few"? You can use PCP to *help yourself*, and all those around you.

Let's wrap up this section with one more little word of suggestion. Call it "grow power," or planting the seed, or both, but there is a sound PCP principle in the Christian concept of *tithing*. The sharing of your bounty with others is essential to steady financial progress. Find some worthy organizations, churches, charities, or needy families and make regular donations in true charity.

If you are short of money at first, give of your time and

energy in loving service. Whatever you give, give it freely like a farmer joyously planting his seed with the full knowledge of the abundance of the harvest. With this approach you will never regress, but go on from riches and wealth to greater and greater opulence.

Points to Remember from This Chapter

1. *Don't confuse effort with results!*
2. Build a launching pad of positive attitudes toward money.
3. Respect the law of attraction and repulsion: *That which you give, or would willingly give, you attract; and that which you withhold, or strongly desire to withhold, you repel.*
4. Train yourself to think and act as a person of great financial resources.
5. Carefully tune your consciousness to the PCP power broadcast.
6. Express your financial desires in terms that are compatible with the PCP principles.
7. Push the PCP "start" button, and daily monitor the flight of your rocket to financial gain.
8. *Let* PCP manifest ever increasing abundance in your life—follow the urges to success as they come to you.

how to
Use PCP to Eliminate
Worry and Gain Serenity

One of the big things that distinguishes man from the lower animals is his tremendous capacity for worry and anxiety. The increasing flow of money the PCP is bringing into your life should be a giant step toward elimination of worry. We will more quickly eliminate worry by improving our understanding of it's nature.

The nature of worry

Let's begin by referring to a dictionary. Mine defines worry as: undue solicitude; vexation; anxiety. An old friend of mine has a more homely, but perhaps clearer description. He calls it borrowing trouble that would best be left undisturbed. Another friend complained that just when things are going well for him, he seems to be literally filled with a vague sense of impending disaster. Fortunately this good man has learned a set of metaphysical techniques to get rid of this feeling before the fear causes real trouble to be manifest in his life. But he will be much more comfortable when he learns to *prevent even the beginnings* of such a terrible experience.

There are many people whose whole lives are tainted by

73

unreasoning fears and anxiety. One of the potentially most efficient secretaries I have ever met was unfortunately a victim of groundless worries. She had a good job as secretary to the sales manager of a growing aerospace corporation. Her boss was having an energetic personality clash with the Marketing Vice President, and she mistook the senior executive's displeasure as being directed at her. When the sales manager resigned in disgust, she unreasonably assumed that she was due to be discharged. So she quit, and took a new job that paid $100 a month less while demanding that she take twice the pressure.

The anxious act of running from a possibility of being fired may seem strange to you, but each of us has reacted just as irrationally over something. We concoct elaborate rationalizations to convince ourselves that we avoided the formal party because we were too tired, or that we turned down the promotion because it meant moving away from our home city, or that we didn't enter the golf club tournament because we were too busy, or etc. Each of these reasons may be true, but they could just as easily be a cover up for some lurking fear of failure. Don't say, "That couldn't possibly apply to me." If you're *sure* it doesn't, I'll give you 100 to 1 it does!

Our buried or hidden fears cause us the most trouble because they manifest in vague or general feelings of discomfort and uneasiness. Let's begin the process of rooting them out along with the readily recognizable ones.

How to build a launch pad to blast off from all worry and anxiety

Understanding is always the foundation of progress. Our foundation, or launch pad in this case, will be built by careful study of your own fear and anxiety patterns. A little old fashioned introspection will be good for what ails you. So we will begin by making a detailed list of everything that disturbs, worries, or bugs you, or even the things which make you slightly uncomfortable. Carry a small packet notebook everywhere you go for a while. Promise yourself that you will be specially sensitive to your every feeling of anxiety, and that you will record each one on the spot for study later when you are relaxed and can be objective.

We will work with a representative list of fears supplied by a former student. Don't be at all embarrassed at the thought of admitting a few fears. Every one who has ever walked on the earth has experienced fear and anxiety. Even the great Inspiration of the Christian religion admitted such feelings: "Then saith he unto them, My soul is exceeding sorrowful, even unto death: tarry ye here, and watch with me. And he went a little further, and fell on his face and prayed, saying, O, my Father, if it be possible, let this cup pass from me. . . ." (Matt. 26:38, 39.) We are told in the next few verses that He prayed these same words on three separate occasions that night. We can surely understand the anxiety of knowing the personal suffering which was to come, and yet being honor bound to accept it.

Here is the sample list of one student's fears:

1. Fear of ridicule resulting in:
   (a) too easily embarrassed
   (b) too shy to speak in front of a group
   (c) hesitant to express a new idea
2. Fear of failure, resulting in:
   (a) afraid to tackle a new project
   (b) worry on the job leading to ineffectiveness
   (c) thinking and acting defensively
3. Fear of the loss of love, resulting in:
   (a) jealousy and possessiveness
   (b) feelings of not being needed or wanted
   (c) feel rejected
   (d) inferiority complex and despondency

4. Fear of bodily harm, resulting in:
   (a) squeamishness about heights
   (b) unreasonably afraid of germs
   (c) tendency to shy away from sharp objects
   (d) fear of torture
   (e) fear of auto accidents
5. Fear of the unknown, resulting in:
   (a) fear of being punished by God
   (b) fear of eternal damnation
   (c) feeling of impending doom
   (d) fear of death
   (e) the nameless terror
6. Special personal fears, like:
   (a) fear of being fired for no reason
   (b) unexplainable fear of a specific person
   (c) fear of starvation
   (d) fear of obesity
   (e) fear of mice, spiders, worms
   (f) discomfort when telling a joke, for fear that no one will get it

Keep adding to your personal list every time you experience any feeling of anxiety or mental discomfort. Ten days will usually be enough time to gather a representative sample of your haunting fears. Next arrange them in patterns or groups of related anxieties as we did in our example.

Gaining a working familiarity with your deep-seated anxiety patterns may take a little longer. Start by examining them one at a time. Ask each one, "Who is your father?" In other words, who or what originally caused this particular fear in me? Question each fear in the silence of your own quiet place, then pause and wait for the answer. An impression or feeling will come to you from the recesses of your mind. The answers may be vague at first, and you may be inclined not to accept them. But stick with the project! Its successful conclusion can be worth much more than years of twice-a-week sessions on the psychiatrist's couch. Most of us are sufficiently well adjusted that psychoanalysis would be of questionable value, but *everyone* has a few lurking anxiety patterns. Thus a reasonable amount of *self analysis* can be the beginning of tremendously improved personal comfort and effectiveness.

Work with your fear list daily to build more and more understanding. Knowledge and experience are the positive antidotes to anxiety and fear. Combine them with proper application of Psycho-Cosmic Power and you can free yourself forever.

How to use PCP to knock your fears down

When you are thoroughly familiar with your anxiety and fear patterns, you are ready to start knocking them off their perch within you, one by one. The simple secret of knocking off a fear is to face it squarely. First admit you have the fear, then you are able to do something about it. Again ask it, "Who is your father?" and carefully study its origin. Next do whatever study and research is necessary to gain a full understanding of the subject matter of the fear. Then look the whole thing squarely in the eye and *do the thing you fear!*

At every point in the study and overcoming of your fears, it will pay to apply your PCP. Use the PCP formula to attract the necessary information and ideas to increase your understanding and dissolve the fear itself. Thousands of people have used these simple principles to rid themselves of haunting fears and energy sapping anxieties.

How a junior executive conquered fear in business

A young executive was horribly afraid to speak before a group. For three weeks in a row he was scheduled to deliver a verbal report to a staff meeting. He was so tied up with anxiety that he became physically ill each time, and had to take to bed instead of addressing the meeting. Now he also became afraid of losing his job, so in desperation he sought assistance. Here was a case where the patient had tried to face up to his fear, but his psychological tools were inadequate to stand alone. While discussing the problem, he began to see that he was plagued with a deep-seated fear of *ridicule*. He had been teased unmercifully for a very funny slip of the tongue while reciting in a first grade class. From that time on, he had been afraid to talk before any kind of a group. By being shy and unobtrusive, he had managed to avoid almost every necessity to talk to more than two people at a time. But now his whole career was at stake! If he didn't smash this fear he would lose all chance for advancement, perhaps for all time.

He began intensive treatments to dissolve this crippling fear. The bold assertion was that the PCP energy was now expressing itself in and through his being, and he could speak anywhere with perfect poise and verbal effectiveness. He constructed a little affirmation to use at every moment of mental pause during his working day:

> The infinite power of the universe is concentrated upon my fear of speaking, dissolving it into the nothingness from which it came. From this moment on, the Psycho-Cosmic Power is expressing through me as poise, relaxation, and effectiveness. I can talk to any group about anything now!"

He faithfully renewed his contact with the PCP energy literally hundreds of times a day for the whole week before the next staff meeting. Then on the morning he was to speak he fortified himself with a mild tranquilizer. We won't say that his eloquence carried away the staff meeting, but he did give his report. The next time he was asked to speak it was a little easier. And now he enjoys expressing himself before any kind of a group. You can overcome any fear or anxiety by the conscientious application of PCP while intelligently facing up to the problem.

A marriage saved by conquering fear

The wife of a young medical doctor began to feel her marriage falling apart. The demands of his growing practice kept the doctor away from home a good part of the time, and she began to suspect that there might be another woman. Thus began a vicious circle of suspicion and accusation that rapidly widened the rift, until her fear of losing the man she loved became nearly an obsession. She had encountered the basic principles of PCP earlier in life, and thought them interesting, but made no special attempt to apply them. Now, feeling there was nothing to lose, she turned to the great power of the Cosmic.

While meditating on her problem, she was led to understand that it was her own actions of jealousy and possessiveness which had driven the wedge between them. She began praying regularly for peace and harmony in her home, and promised herself to be friendly and understanding to her husband at all times. It was far from easy to choke down the feelings of loneliness, and smile at her husband when he left on an emergency call, but she forced herself to do just that.

Her heartfelt prayers combined with her change of attitude to lessen the tension for both of them almost immediately. After a week of the new atmosphere they were able to sit down quietly and discuss their problems without yelling at each other. Their combined effort finally rooted out the tension and replaced it with deeper understanding and mutual trust, and they are a happy married couple today.

Overcoming your fears and anxieties will certainly work to

the benefit of every area of your life. We will turn our attention next to a more detailed plan to use PCP to eliminate your fears in an orderly and effective manner.

Points to Remember from This Chapter

1. Worry is the borrowing of trouble that would best be left undisturbed.

2. Make a sample list of your own fears, so that you may study and eliminate them.

3. Fear is overcome by knowledge, familiarity, and by facing up to it.

4. Others, in case histories in this chapter, have used PCP to eliminate fears with great success. So can you.

how to

Make a Workable Plan for Eliminating All Your Fear, Worry, and Anxiety

In our last chapter we worked with the basic principles necessary to rid ourselves of fear, worry, and anxiety. The next step is to formulate a workable plan for the systematic and effective elimination of these destroyers of happiness and efficiency. We hinted at the key to this earlier, but now let's face it head-on in detail.

The key is honest self-acceptance

Our scientists and engineers are quick to tell us that proper definition of a problem is the biggest single step toward its solution. In this case we must face the hard fact that we are something less than perfect individuals in our personal manifestation of life here and now. Whether we like it or not, we came into this life with certain strengths and *weaknesses*, and we have developed some more of *each* as the years carried us along. First take an objective look at the sum total of the entity which is *you*, and then *accept it* as thoroughly suitable raw

81

material from which to build an ever-improving life expression.

For deep psychological reasons, the ability to accept one's self is intricately bound up in the need for overcoming mankind's most disastrous fear: fear of that abstract and woefully unknown principle which most men call God. By brooding about its many weaknesses, mistakes, and shortcomings, mankind as a whole has developed a guilt consciousness. The collective subconscious mind erroneously assumes that the Infinite Creator of our planet must be horrendously displeased with the outcome of its creative efforts. This collective feeling impinges on men and naturally makes them uncomfortable. So they build little mental walls around it and try to ignore it, or at least isolate it from their moment to moment thought life. But this very repression of the feeling drives it deeper within our beings where it can tap the very source of our vitality and use it against us.

Look at the problem honestly: every human being has some degree of feelings of insecurity, inadequacy, unworthiness, and the fear of impending punishment for past mistakes. When a small setback or a full-fledged tragedy strikes our experience, our first instinct is to wail, "What have I done to deserve this?" We live our whole lives like the two-year-old who was fascinated by the pretty red color of his mother's lipstick. He was completely taken aback when he was spanked for using the lipstick to decorate the living room wall. He had no feeling of wrongdoing while exhibiting his lipstick artistry, thus the punishment made him feel totally insecure—anything he might do could result in the manifested wrath of his only known source of security, love, and care, *his mother.*

It is this same childish lack of perspective that imputes wrath to our concept of Deity, or Cosmic Goodness and that causes resentment or fear of policemen. This is simply fear of punishment for unknown or long-forgotten transgressions. As children, we all committed some kind of minor infraction of the adult-established rules of behavior, and forgot about it, only to be severely chastised later. Now if mother or father, who represent all love and authority, can carry a grudge and punish us for something we had honestly forgotten, how much more must we believe that our concept of a "Heavenly Father" who is omniscient is capable of the same sort of grudge-carrying only on a much larger scale.

Thus the natural result of our childishly conditioned re-action is a terrible fear of our own conception of God, or Deity. We can never truly accept ourselves with all our obvious shortcomings, until we somehow get over the unreasoning fears generated by the concept of God as an omniscient mother-father combination bent on punishing us for not being perfect. Let's take a closer look at the Cosmic idea of God, and work to gain a more mature understanding of ourselves. We must make this understanding reach our heart and our subconscious, not just our little conditioned intellect!

A closer Cosmic look at Deity in our lives

The intelligent concept of "first cause" or "unmoved mover" seems a reasonable starting place. To any thinking individual, the vastness of our Cosmic universe and the intricacy of the details which make it up are far beyond anything that one could shrug off as a colossal accident. It is obvious, even to the relatively limited human intellect, that there must be an Infinite Intelligence back of the whole of the manifested universe. And it logically follows that there is an infinite power-substance which manifests under the direction of this Infinite Intelligence. The metaphysician puts it more colorfully when he states that original creation is a result of the self-contemplation of spirit, and it is only the continued self-contemplation of spirit (or Deity if you prefer) which sustains the material world and thus life as we know it. But what are these words really saying? Isn't it clear they mean that you and I, and our whole world of experience, are indeed the creation or manifestation of that same thing, Cosmic Good or God? And isn't the power-substance which provides the vehicles you call your body and mind also an integral part of God?

Brushing aside the childish idea of human weakness and desire to punish that has erroneously been placed on Deity, how have we personally observed God, or Cosmic Intelligence, to act? In this sense we must answer that the Infinite Intelligence which created the universe always acts consistently, according to what is called "natural law." We realize that on those occasions when we thought we saw someone violating a natural law with impunity, (without punishment) it was only the operation of a higher natural law which we did not yet understand. *But the same law will work for us when we use it properly!* It is necessary only to gain that priceless commodity called *understanding.*

If God only works through consistent natural Cosmic laws, and if we agree that we are indeed "His Own" creations, how can we cling to the idea of punishment inconsistently meted out by the Universal Being? The thought becomes an outrageous affront to our intelligence! Fine! But now we must root it out of its hiding places in our subconscious thought patterns, and wash away all the spots where it has colored our thinking and acting. We must understand in the deepest parts of our being that natural Cosmic law carries no grudges! You can wire your doorbell wrong a hundred times, but the laws of electricity won't hold it against you. And when you finally wire it properly, it will work immediately. There is no punishment anywhere in the universe: only the immediate consequences of our proper or improper use of natural law.

Now we can accept ourselves, including all our shortcomings. So you *are* less than perfect! You can decide now to change what you can, and as quickly as possible. In the meantime it is normal and reasonable to *accept yourself exactly as you are.* You know now that the universe accepts you just as you are, so join it! It is only after you have honestly accepted yourself that you can formulate a meaningful plan to eliminate all fear, worry and anxiety. Let's use what we have learned to plan your course to freedom.

How to make a PERT chart for eliminating all fear

In Chapter 6 we suggested making a list of your fears for study, familiarity, and finally elimination. Now we are ready to mould your personal list into a PERT Chart for the orderly elimination of the whole batch of fears. Keeping in mind that the strong fears tend to amplify their weaker counterparts, arrange your list into two sequences: one in order of apparent ease of elimination, and the other in order of relative importance to you. From the perspective gained in this way, we can construct our Chart. For our example we will use the list of fears made by a junior accountant. We picked a short list to simplify the discussion, but your comprehensive list can be handled in exactly the same manner.

List 1. SAMPLE LIST OF FEARS IN ORDER OF IMPORTANCE TO THE INDIVIDUAL

1. Fear of career failure.
2. Fear of financial lack.
3. Feeling of impending disaster.
4. Discomfort when meeting new people.
5. Fear of loss of spouse's love.
6. Fear of expressing new ideas to supervisor.

7. Fear of policemen.
8. Fear of automobile accidents.
9. Fear of being a poor joke teller.
10. Terrified of the darkness.
11. Uncomfortable when thinking about God and Cosmic Justice.

List 2. SAMPLE LIST OF FEARS IN ORDER OF APPARENT EASE OF ELIMINATION

1. Uncomfortable when thinking about God and Cosmic Justice.
2. Terrified of darkness.
3. Feeling of impending disaster.
4. Fear of financial lack.
5. Fear of career failure.
6. Fear of automobile accidents.
7. Fear of policemen.
8. Discomfort when meeting new people.
9. Fear of loss of spouse's love.
10. Fear of expressing new ideas to supervisor.
11. Fear of being a poor joke teller.

The second list grows out of your increasing familiarity with your fears and their interrelatedness, from the work we started in Chapter 6. Our next object is to blend our two lists into a workable PERT chart that will show us the critical path to accomplishment of *freedom from all fear*. Figure 4 shows what the student did with his own list. The chart is simply stated in terms of the goals involved in eliminating his psychological discomforts.

Note that the critical path bowls its way through groups of interrelated fears, like a perfect strike ball. It pinpoints the major areas of concentration, and leaves the lesser fears to be mopped up as a result of the overcoming of just a few major ones. Now you try it. Make your own PERT Chart for the

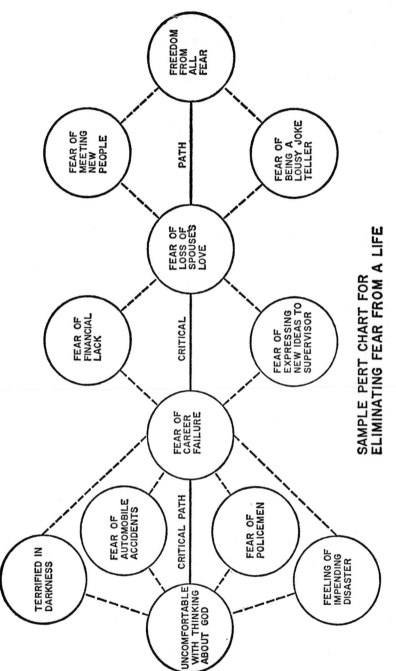

SAMPLE PERT CHART FOR
ELIMINATING FEAR FROM A LIFE

Figure 4.

elimination of all your fears and anxiety. Don't be dismayed if things seem to stay jumbled up at first. The simple act of applying your attention to the problem will lead to its reasonable solution, more quickly than you dare expect. A beginning is much more important than absolute perfection of form. There may be hundreds of possible configurations for your personal chart, but *any* plan is better than no plan at all. And it is your prerogative to revise it as often as the spirit moves you.

The importance of perseverance

On a NASA PERT Chart there would be required completion dates assigned for each box, with carefully detailed scheduling in terms of the critical path. At this stage you may not feel qualified to put dates on your chart; but some sort of an approximate schedule will help you marshall your energies in working the solution.

The technique is to focus your PCP energies on the first box along your critical path. Face up to your problem as we discussed in Chapter 6, and work on it with all the psychic and PCP energy you can muster. Study it, do it over and over, live it, and feel your growing mastery over it—until finally *you know you are free.*

Perseverance is our watchword in this undertaking. The basic purpose of the chart is to point out the sub-goals which have "slack" (more time in the schedule than is actually required for completion), and their relationship to the other sub-goals which form the critical path. If we are not aware of their relative importance to our schedule, the slightest setback of any goal would cause us anxiety. Now we can react to minor setbacks by reshuffling our task priorities, but without the old feelings of discouragement.

Accomplishment always comes from the consistent *applica-*

tion of sound principles according to an intelligently ordered plan. You have studied the principles and made your plan. Success is now merely a matter of staying with it. Keep on and on and on and on—*until you taste sweet victory!* Feel all your old fears and anxiety melting back into the nothingness of their origin. You will begin to experience a growing sense of tranquility or inner peace which nothing can take away from you.

How to enjoy your life of inner peace

You should begin to notice all sorts of happy "fallout." One of the first bits will be the increasing effectiveness of your thinking and working faculties as they become less hampered by the morass of fear and anxiety. And in turn your increasing effectiveness will help you eliminate more of the remnants of the old anxiety patterns.

As we successfully sweep our old fears aside, we make room for that happy state called *peace of mind* or *serenity*. However, a closer look at peace of mind will reveal that it is not merely the absence of worry and anxiety. It is like a tender plant, grown in the clearing left by the elimination of fear, but it grows only where it is planted. When it has grown up straight and strong, it will support the whole superstructure of your cosmic life—then *nothing based in fear can shake you!*

Serenity can never come from inaction! It is a product of planned and orderly action that knows where it is going, and *knows it will succeed.* Everywhere you look, you see the basic forces of nature urging growth and expansion. Peace naturally rewards the creatures who cooperate with nature's driving force. We will have much more to say about following nature's (or spirit's) urgings. It is the real key to unfolding career, richness of experience, fullness and meaning to life. But for now we will settle for one simple example of the value of correctly following that nagging little feeling deep within your being.

How "nervous stomach" was conquered

A young college graduate was in the first few months of his first real job. He had married just after graduation, and now it appeared that a family was on the way. He had been a good student, and was embarked on what looked like a promising career, but he suffered from two problems that somehow seemed to be connected. He developed a "nervous stomach" that gave him fits of nausea at the slightest sign of stress, and he was haunted by the feeling that there is no real meaning to life.

As part of the requirements of his job, he joined a local service club. At a luncheon meeting a speaker hinted of the truths you are reading in this book. Our young man was led by a series of "happy coincidences" to seek books and lectures that brought home the meaning of orienting one's self with the power of the universe. In a matter of months, he was completely cured of his nervous stomach by the self-confidence which grew out of his new-found path of spiritual striving in Cosmic Truth. He has since weathered many successful years of the ups and downs of business and domestic life without a physical problem, because he regularly takes the trouble to insure his continuing peace of mind through study and striving for spiritual growth in Cosmic Truth.

Growth in Cosmic Intelligence is the only assurance of your continuing peace of mind. Let this simple fact guide you to paths of eternal peace and true serenity.

Points to Remember from This Chapter

1. The key to overcoming fear is *self-acceptance.*
2. It is our childish lack of perspective that imputes the quality of wrath or desire to punish us to Deity, or Cosmic Good.

3. God works through natural Cosmic law, and natural laws carry no grudges.

4. Make your own PERT Chart for eliminating all fear. Then follow it consistently to freedom from fear from whatever source.

5. Your perseverance along the Cosmic path will bring you sweet victory over all fear.

6. Your peace of mind, is a result of Cosmic growth *as you plan it*.

how to

Find Your Path to Dynamic Health

Dynamic, physical health is a fascinating paradox. When we have it, we take it for granted; but when it turns into pain or immobility, we realize it is our most priceless inheritance. The physical body is of prime importance to existence in the world of three-dimensional experience, for without it we would be incapable of Cosmic manifestation in tangible form. Few things improve our morale as much as waking up to vibrant health; paradoxically, few things injure good health as much as poor mental attitudes. The value of good health is obvious to all, but the path to its attainment is quite another story.

The materialistic view of your body

The majority of people in our Western civilization take an essentially materialistic view of the body. They are not at all sure about existence (if any) after the change called death, but they are convinced that the body is a three-dimensional, material object which is totally subject to the laws of wear and tear. They "know" that it is subject to accidents and diseases, and that it deteriorates with age.

In short, Occidental (Western civilization) man views his body as an intricate chemical plant, completely dependent on the physical inputs of food, water, and occasional medicines for its well being. Many interesting fads and theories have grown out of this position, and some of them have merit. One school of physical culture believes "You are what you eat." This is a reasonable sounding hypothesis which leads to an increased interest in good nutrition that is bound to be beneficial. The most single-minded materialists of today would not argue against the substance of the growing field of psychosomatic medicine (the influence of the emotions on physical health) but as a whole way of life it is considerably out of balance. It's true that if you consider thoughts and emotions as *mental and emotional food,* then the expanded idea of *you are what you eat* comes closer to explaining the path of health as it is. But there are other significant ideas to be carefully considered also.

The art and science of medicine has "Come of age" in our century. The scientific study of anatomy, and marvelous advances in the field of organic chemistry have been combined by modern medicine to greatly extend our average life span. Newly discovered hormones are prescribed for health improvement and even birth control, special vitamin preparations relieve everything from nervousness and lack of energy to excessive bleeding, and we are helped by tranquilizers, pep pills, pain pills, antibiotics, anti-depressants and diuretics. There are even psychedelic pills purported to be able to carry us on a mystic trip all the way to heaven. Each drug may be good in its place, but each also has its dangers and "side effects." Thus medical scientists are ardent in their study of "body chemistry," seeking to understand and explain everything in terms of electrolytic balance or the "genetic" code by which cells reproduce whole bodies from the information contained in the chromosomes and genes of one tiny embryo.

The passage of time serves to enhance the inevitable progress of the body of knowledge we call medical science. Its dedicated researchers press on toward new antibiotics and new knowledge which will lead to the overcoming of more killer diseases. This is all necessary and good, but it leaves out a whole Cosmic dimension. We have passed through the dark period when men considered the body alone. Now most thinking people look upon the complex of mind-body as the entity needing treatment. Psychiatry and tranquilizers seem to be the hallmark of our new culture. And at that it's certainly a step up from the days of the "I am my body and nothing else" cults of popular thought. Yes, medicine has finally added the fourth dimension of mind to the three physical dimensions, but it has another whole one to go before it can treat the whole being. The missing element is the life force, the Cosmic Force itself, which comes in through the dimension of spirit or soul as the entry point into our existence on the earth plane.

The spiritual and Cosmic view of you as a person

There is a fascinating combination of the old and new in the true spiritual concept, of a sum total of you as a person. Let's begin with the aerospace industry's *systems engineering* approach. Much of our great space-age success springs from the systems engineering technique of visualizing the complete entity (or system) needed to accomplish a given mission, and then breaking it down into working sub-systems and further subdivisions. Thus work can proceed along a PERT Chart path to the final accomplishment of the mission.

It was a similar approach which lead the ancient spiritual seers and sages to view a human being as a complete entity. Naturally they recognized the physical body and the mind, but they also realized that this was much less than the whole of the

entity. The Cosmic life-giving force that animates and moti-
vates each of us is not to be found within the confines of a
physical body, or even within the less definable something
psychologists call the mind. There are "bodies" beyond the
limits of the physical, but we will go into this in a later
chapter. Right now we will confine our systems engineering
definition of a human being to a *Cosmic spirit or soul, expressing as a composite "whole being" through mental, emotional
and physical "bodies."*

There may be some who still question the validity of the
concept of a human soul. When you meet such a "doubter,"
help him reach a new understanding with this simple but
modern analogy. Modern industry is characterized by more
and more sophisticated machines. For instance: the *numerical
control*, or computer operated milling machine exhibits nearly
human versatility and adaptations. It turns out widely divergent sizes and shapes of complicated precision parts when
its operator feeds a punched paper tape into its computer,
inserts the tools and work, and pushes the "start" button. It is
altogether reasonable to equate the milling machine to your
physical body, and its computer to your mind. Then comes the
logical question: who programs the computer? Or more simply, who prepares the punched paper tape that tells the computer how to direct the machine? You, as the human program-
mer, stand in the same relationship to the numerical controlled
machine as your Cosmic soul does to your mind-body complex.

Certainly the operator-programmer needs his machine-
computer complex. Without it he would have no way to create
good precision parts. In the same way, your soul needs its mind-
body complex if it is to manifest in the three dimensional world
and carry out its business of evolution. Let's carry the analogy
one step forward. When the operator pushes the "start" button,
the electric current flows into and energizes the system which

then makes the parts under the direction of the computer. The electric energy that drives the machine is brought in through wires from a distant power source.

Now what is the energy that drives your body? It is the abstract thing we call *emotion.* Someone will surely say, "That's ridiculous! Everybody knows it's the food we eat that supplies our energy." And it is true that food might be considered the fuel which is burned in the engine that drives the generator. But without the generator itself, there would be only waste matter. Now—it is our emotions that we must compare to the generator. Skeptical? Read on!

Remember the surge of energy that came with your last piece of really good news? Or the vanishing fatigue at the spur of the moment suggestion of an informal get together? Or ski trip? Or bowling? Medical doctors tell us that our excitement causes the secretion of extra adrenaline which gives us new strength and vigor, but there is much more to it than a simple physical secretion. In a later chapter we will study the emotional "body" and the way it brings electrical-life energy to the physical shell through the sympathetic nervous system, but right now we will proceed with our Cosmic and spiritual view of you as a complex person.

The spiritual view sees all causation as coming from the higher stages of existence, down to the lower. Thus you might visualize the Cosmic life energy as flowing from the soul through the mind (or mental body), on through the emotions (or emotional body) to the physical vehicle your friends recognize as *you* when you pass them on the street.

From this viewpoint, it is clear that *all* physical disorders and disease must originate on the mental and emotional levels. No one would doubt that the mind-emotion complex is capable of producing negative effects on the physical body. The whole field of psychosomatic medicine is founded on that premise.

For instance, where would our doctors get toward fighting ulcers of the stomach without tranquilizers to help reduce nervousness and tension while striving to help nature repair the physical damages? In both *The Miraculous Laws of Universal Dynamics* and *Helping Yourself with E.S.P.*, I set out a table of mental-emotional causes and their general physical effects. At the risk of being redundant, I want to present the table again here, with only very minor revisions. Its purpose is not to help you diagnose the causes of specific ailments, but to dramatize the reality of the mind-emotion to physical body cause and effect relationship. The table should be taken more as descriptive direction than unyielding fact, but a good long look will help you to better understand what we do to ourselves with our thought-emotions in negative patterns.

Although this may seem like a terrible threat of disaster from the mere act of harboring a few negative thought patterns, students of both metaphysics and psychosomatic medicine would agree that there is much truth in it. Guard your habitual thought patterns as the best way to prevent physical problems—before your thinking has crystallized into objective, physical manifestation.

In all fairness to our materialist friends, we must admit that, speaking from the world of normal experience, there must be a few purely physical causes of physical disorders. I am reminded of an anecdote often repeated by one of my favorite teachers. It went something like this: The voice on my telephone said, "Reverend, I have a needle stuck in my leg. Will you please pray for me?" To which I replied, "Of course not. Pull it out!"

Even the greatest of our metaphysical teachers, Jesus of Nazareth, taught care in the use of the concept that thought controls everything: *Which of you by taking thought can add one cubit unto his stature?* (Matt. 6:27.)

In the beginning of this section we hinted at our clue to the best approach. We have borrowed it from the aerospace industry.

TABLE OF MENTAL POISONS AND THEIR SYMPTOMS

Poisonous Mental Patterns	*Resulting Symptoms*
1. Resentment, bitterness, hatred.	Skin rash, boils, acne, blood disorders, cancer, allergies, heart trouble, stiff joints.
2. Confusion, frustration, anger.	Common cold, pneumonia, tuberculosis; emphysema, disorders of the respiratory tract, asthma; eye, ear, nose and throat trouble.
3. Anxiety, impatience, greed.	High blood pressure, migraine headaches, ulcers, nearsightedness, hard of hearing, heart attacks.
4. Cynicism, pessimism, defeatism.	Low blood pressure, anemia, polio, diabetes, leprosy, low income, kidney disorders.
5. Revulsion, fear, guilt.	Accidents, cancer, personal failure, poverty, poor sex, "tired blood."
6. Antagonism, inferiority, introversion.	Allergies, recurring headaches, lack of friends, heart murmur, accident prone.

How to use the systems engineering type of approach to heal your whole being

The systems engineering approach naturally takes the entire entity into account. Thus it is the balanced program which seeks to heal the whole being. As we would expect, it is practical and logical in sequence, seeking to get *maximum relief from the minimum effort.*

In aggravated cases, begin by relieving the physical symptoms by usual means available. Take aspirin for your headache, or tranquilizers for your nervousness, or anything else that will bring some immediate relief. It will be good to apply PCP to the symptoms as early as possible—then it may not be necessary to seek material help. Use our standard PCP formula to begin a natural renewal of the tissues or nerves in the affected area. Let's refer back to the spiritual concept of your being to be sure that you are not accepting some negative conditions as "incurable." *There is absolutely no health condition that can withstand your PCP when it is applied on a sound systems engineering basis!*

So far we have accepted the normal physical aids to pain relief, and added only the use of PCP to begin healing and renewal. Psycho-Cosmic Power can and will heal any condition. But if you don't root out the mental-emotional cause and break the offending thought-reaction pattern, your problem is apt to recur as an even more terrible manifestation than the one you eliminated. In Chapters 6 and 7 we developed techniques for ridding your being of fear and worry, and for obtaining true peace of mind. The very process of gaining peace of mind will certainly have a positive effect on your health, but you can do much more by extending the same techniques.

Start with the existing physical symptoms. Ask each distressing symptom, "Who is your father? What negative thought pattern spawned you?" Work with this question until your lurking negative thought-reaction patterns are all brought into the light of observation and understanding. Then, just as you did for gaining peace of mind, use your PCP to root out and destroy the patterns of negativity by your adherence to Cosmic Truths—and *replace them with healthy, positive patterns.*

A healing of financial insecurity

A widow in her late fifties developed a serious heart condition that seemed to top off a series of minor ailments of the liver, bladder, throat, and gall bladder. A short consultation revealed that her anxiety-fear pattern was financial in nature. A combination of greed and lack of some business judgment had led her into a venture which was way over her head. Now she was terribly afraid that she would lose her whole fortune and "spend the rest of my life in the poorhouse." To one whose life had always contained an abundance of the material luxuries, this fear was even greater than the fear of death. It was quite easy to relieve the physical symptoms by application of the PCP energies through a process of laying on of the hands, but rooting out the cause was another matter. We were able to control all physical symptoms by twice-daily treatments with the PCP power, but new conditions kept trying to break out until a great deal of prayer and educational effort helped restore a measure of financial security. As soon as the financial crisis was passed, she noticed no further physical problems.

How to build your launch pad to perfect health

The systems engineering approach also gives us the basis for building our launch pad to perfect health. We will start with the physical and work back to the mental-emotional balance which prevents new outbreaks of trouble. Let's do this in four steps:

1. *Eliminate habits which are detrimental to health.*
Sometimes in the midst of the pressure and confusion of

daily living, we forget the simple rules of caring for the physical body. Promise yourself that you will never let any circumstance or situation cause you to maltreat or neglect your body. Then avoid all forms of overindulgence. Many things that are relaxing and enjoyable in reasonable quantities can become real poisons when taken in excess. Food, alcohol, tobacco, coffee, tea, salt, and even exercise can make us miserable when we take more than our reasonable share at any one point in time. Different people have widely different tolerances for these pleasures and necessities. Study your capacity for each—then enjoy your share, but don't overdo!

2. *Develop positive health habits.*

To break an undesirable habit, it is easier to replace it with a positive habit than to try to leave only a vacuum. Make a concerted effort to establish good health habits. Pay attention to proper nutrition, get regular exercise, and enough rest. A few simple muscle stretching and breathing exercises each day will contribute more to your general physical well-being than pounds of medicines and synthetic vitamins. Think health, and act in the obvious ways to protect it, but don't overdo that either!

3. *Eliminate negative thought-emotion patterns.*

Review the table of mental poisons and their symptoms with the idea of becoming sensitive to the thought-emotion patterns that cause so much of our trouble. Except for the obvious results of overindulgence or neglect, all physical problems can be traced to one negative thought-reaction pattern or another. You can't afford the effects of harboring these poisonous emotions! So root out every one of them, *now!* And remember, even though resentment or hatred may be completely "justified," it is equally as destructive to your health as if the whole thing were your own fault. Meditate on this important truth, then *act accordingly!*

4. *Develop strong, positive thought-emotion patterns.*

Again, it is easier to break bad habits by replacing them with good ones. It will help every area of your life to begin developing powerful habits of optimism, of a regular and infectious smile, and a bright and happy greeting to every person you meet. No better health advice was ever given to man than the immortal words of St. Paul: *Finally, brethren, whatsoever things are true, whatsoever things are honest, whatsoever things are just, whatsoever things are pure, whatsoever things are lovely, whatsoever things are of good report; if there be any virtue, and if there be any praise, think on these things* (Phil. 4:8.) This is positive Cosmic advice upon which to launch your better health and develop it consistently toward perfect health.

Points to Remember from This Chapter

1. You are a spiritual being, expressing as a composite whole the Cosmic Wisdom, including mental, emotional, and physical bodies.

2. The Cosmic life energy flows from the spirit through the mind and emotions to the physical body.

3. All disease and disorder originates on the mental or emotional level.

4. The systems engineering approach can be effectively used to heal your whole being.

5. Build your launching pad to work toward perfect health:
   (1) Replace habits detrimental to health with positive health habits.
   (2) Replace negative thought-emotion patterns with strong, positive patterns with the force of your Cosmic Powers as directed in this book.

how to

Attain Ideal Health
for Yourself and Your
Loved Ones

Most people who continually suffer from physical problems say they want to be healed—but somewhere inside themselves they believe that healing is impossible for them. Chronic sufferers of bad health quickly accept the fact that they will suffer for the rest of their life. And they get just what they expect! It's high time we open our minds to the proposition that no *health condition is absolutely incurable!*

But any condition you *believe* to be incurable will remain so for the simple reason that you cease to seek your healing. A bit of sound advice was left us by the Master Healer in his oft-quoted, but seldom really believed statement: *Ask, and it shall be given you; seek, and ye shall find; knock, and it shall be opened unto you: for everyone that asketh receiveth; and he that seeketh findeth; and to him that knocketh it shall be opened.* (Matt. 7:7, 8.) This indeed is an expression of Cosmic Power.

A healing of the lungs described

A good friend of ours recently consulted several medical doctors about a serious health problem. Each doctor informed him he was suffering from the "incurable" disease, emphysema, and recommended his leaving the Los Angeles area in favor of a drier, smog-free climate. Such a move was designed to "alleviate his suffering somewhat, and prolong his life a few months." But this man is a good student of Cosmic metaphysics, so he refused to accept the doctors' sentence of exile and death. When he came to our house to talk it over, my wife Eileen offered to assist by prayer and the application of the PCP energy through the laying on of hands. They embarked on a joint program to eliminate the mental causes while healing the symptoms. They relieved the congestion almost immediately, and the *healing was complete* in less than a month as verified by a doctor. Our friend is even smoking again with no discomfort, and he is sure there will be no further outbreaks.

How to use PCP to heal your friends and loved ones

The launching pad concept is as important to the healing of another as to yourself. If you are to be really successful in bringing permanent healing to someone, you must secure his cooperation in building some kind of mental launching platform. In other words, you must begin by changing the patient's mental attitudes and reaction patterns. Chronic arthritis sufferers may take aspirin tablets four or five times a day for relief, but they know they will need more in a few hours. Any relief is better than no help at all, but we will be much more effective if we concentrate on bringing those major mental and physical changes that result in eradication of the cause as well as the symptoms.

It makes a lot of sense to develop the attitude that *pain is one of nature's greatest blessings*. It warns us of trouble while there is still time to do something about it. Imagine a completely pain-free world for a moment. At first it seems wonderful to contemplate, but when you start visualizing masses of people dropping dead because their warning systems failed to indicate that some part of the body needed attention, the idea quickly looses its glamour. Pain should be eliminated only after its causes have been determined and a positive program for healing the whole entity has been established.

A little reflection will show that the best healing work you can do is the regular teaching of healthy thought-emotion-reaction patterns to your family and every person you contact. In this type of teaching an old bromide hits the point perfectly: *Actions speak louder than words!* Particularly when we are striving to teach sound spiritual thinking and reacting, it is our *example* that gains the attention. *Every time* you *lose your temper, you are saying to those around you, "This is my true belief of the way individuals should act!"* Similarly, every time you return kindness for abuse, you are demonstrating your understanding of the truth of the Master's injunction: *Ye have heard that it hath been said, "An eye for an eye, and a tooth for a tooth." But I say unto you, that ye resist not evil; but whosoever shall smite thee on thy right cheek, turn him the other also. And if any man will sue thee at the law, and take away thy coat, let him have thy cloke also. And whosoever shall compel thee to go a mile, go with him twain. Give to him that asketh thee, and from him that would borrow of thee turn not away. Ye have heard that it hath been said, "Thou shall love thy neighbor, and hate thy enemy." But I say unto you, love your enemies, bless them that curse you, do good for them which despitefully use you, and persecute you; that ye may be children of your Father which is in heaven: for he maketh his sun to rise on the evil and on the good, and sendeth rain on the just and on the unjust.* (Matt. 5:38–45.)

All this as set out above may sound like a tremendously big order for you to do, but it is the Cosmic secret of all mental and physical health. Only a dunderhead would take this as a complete course of action for the material world. If we did so, then a Hitler or Mao Tse Tung would certainly be ruling the whole world. Of course there is a time to be firm and fight if necessary for our family and way of life, *but* that is not to say we should act or fight with hatred or resentment in our hearts! We must approach our material lives with balance and judgment, and there is *never* a time to let negative emotions cloud our reason or fill our systems with poison. A soft, firm voice will win many more arguments than all the ranting and raving you might muster.

We haven't strayed so far from the healing of others as you might think. Two thousand years ago a Man came to earth to teach healing through compassion, love, and often the laying on of hands. Along with His perfect example of healing the "incurable" diseases of his day, He left us a great challenge: *Verily, verily, I say unto you, he that believeth on me, the works that I do shall he do also; and greater works than these shall he do. . . .* Those of us who profess to be His followers must admit that we are hypocrites *unless we seek to bring cosmic healing "miracles" to every sufferer we meet!*

How shall you bring healing to people? First notice the deeply spiritual tone we have tried to set for this section. Healing of the sort we are discussing comes only from Cosmic Spirit—but from Spirit working with the invocation and assistance of a human channel. Wherever possible you should gain the cooperation of your patient. Explain what you intend to accomplish, and use PCP together to eliminate the symptoms and mental-emotional causes. There is much power in joining with another in scientific prayer. That's what PCP is all about. Look at this promise of the Master: *Again I say unto you, that if two of you shall agree on earth as touching anything that they shall ask, it shall be done for them of my Father which is in heaven. For where two or three are gathered together in my name, there am I in the midst of them.* (Matt. 18:19–20.)

In many of the healing "miracles" described in the Bible, Jesus touched or laid hands on the patient. Following this example in an unbroken chain from the Apostles to the present day, practitioners of the healing art have healed with prayer and the laying on of hands. In our own healing work, my wife and I both use the hands for the direction of the life giving Cosmic energies which we "see" and feel while performing our personal healing services. Different healers develop techniques of their own to get maximum results, but all apply the PCP energies to the patient in one way or another. Those who are interested in greater detail of suggested healing techniques will find a whole chapter in my earlier book, *Helping Yourself with E.S.P.*

What shall you do if your patient cannot or will not be present? Do your best! The PCP energies will always respond to your positive direction. Visualize them flowing into your patient's body and mind: cleansing, healing, and revitalizing every part and area of the life. Make it a habit to send the healing energies to your patient twice each day as part of your own meditation periods. If you keep yourself tuned to the PCP frequency, it takes only a few seconds to direct this omnipotent force to help someone else. And the mental effort of "praying" on a Cosmic Level for someone else cannot help but bless you in the ways you need it most.

How to use PCP to heal yourself

My experience has been that people are generally more effective healers when working for the healing of others than for themselves. It is much easier to visualize the PCP energies cleansing and healing someone else. You can turn them loose with faith and love, and then forget about it until time for the next treatment. But when we work for ourselves, we have the tendency to examine the pain every few minutes to see if we are making any progress. This is about as useful as digging up flower seeds in your garden every few minutes to see if they are sprouting well. The result is the same in each case—ABSO-LUTELY NO PROGRESS.

When you are the one who needs the healing, it is more important than usual that you renew your tuning in on the PCP source. Intone the mystic mantra, and claim your oneness with the infinity of the PCP power. Feel the Cosmic energy surging through your being, and know the joy of it.

This time it should be easy to express your desire in terms of the nature of PCP. Certainly the life-giving Cosmic Power wants to express through you as perfect health, vitality, and effectiveness. The same vital forces that grew your body from the pattern furnished in one tiny germ cell can repair or replace any damaged or diseased part. It is simply a matter of *believing* that a perfect healing is possible, and *applying* the PCP energy to the task with vigor and joyous expectation.

How scabs from an accident disappeared

An elderly woman experienced a disastrous automobile accident which left her face a mass of nasty scabs. Her husband was concerned for her morale more than her appearance, so he invited her to join him in using PCP to obtain a perfect healing. They treated the injured face together twice each day, claiming that the PCP power was restoring it to perfection of form with no trace of a scar. One evening, just as he was telling her that her face would come out perfect, the entire scab tissue suddenly fell off her face. He told me, "It looked like her whole face was falling off, but underneath was beautiful new pink skin without a mark on it!" There is no limit to the healing power of PCP, but YOU must set the process in motion by applying it with the *happy expectation of perfect results*.

Let's take just a moment to examine the expression of your

desire that is most compatible with PCP. We must realize that the infinite life force of the universe is constantly seeking to express more and more of itself. Like any other force in nature, it will act or move along the lines of least resistance. Just as water always flows downhill, and electricity flows with greatest energy where the resistance of the conductor is least; so the life force will surge with greatest power where the conditions are most favorable to its manifestation. Therefore your desire should always be couched within the framework of expressing ever more life, vitality, and quality of beingness.

How to communicate PCP for health

Seek always to discover new ways of improving your quality of expression of the life force. Talk to your inner self; tell it you seek perfect health as part of your overall program to cooperate with the infinite life force in manifesting ever improving quality in the whole of your existence. If you have an ailment or suffer from some physical deficiency, you owe it to yourself and the infinite life force to use PCP to obtain perfect health. Joyfully accept the help of the greatest power in the universe, and *know* that it desires your healing as much as you do.

This is the point where your finger is firmly placed on the PCP "start" button. The countdown is simplicity itself. Certainly your desire for perfect health is compatible with the PCP principle, so it is only necessary to quickly check your attitude and faith. Do you believe that PCP can help you? Do you feel the power flowing through your being? Do you feel your desire transferring to the Cosmic Force? Wonderful! Now give the firing command. Repeat the following, aloud if possible, with full expectation of Cosmic Good:

I direct the Psycho-Cosmic Power to heal my body now. I feel it flowing into my being, dissolving everything that is unlike the perfection of the life giving principle, cleansing every

particle of my body and leaving it completely whole and in perfect health. I give thanks for my perfect healing now.

Then relax and monitor your progress, but without "digging up the seeds" to see if they are sprouting. On the first PCP application one woman completely healed a skin rash that had bothered her for months, and a young man had a small wart simply drop off, leaving no trace of its former existence. Sometimes, results are not instantaneous, but you should approach each application of PCP as the only time you need apply it to your problem. Expect good results, but never be discouraged if you don't see an immediate manifestation. Some healings come in the form of gradual growth or strengthening of the afflicted part, and others may spring full grown into manifestation sometime between the first and ten thousandth application. Perseverance and faith, with twice-daily application of PCP, will bring perfect healing to anything you dare seek to heal!

How to protect yourself and your loved ones from all harm

A useful concept to consider from modern psychology is the firmly established idea that some people are "accident prone." In other words, psychologists recognize that some people actually attract accidents and similar misfortunes by the action of their personalities on their environment. One friend of mine exhibited this tendency to an extreme. Her life seemed to be one continuous string of "freak" accidents and bodily infections. A little analysis showed that each accident served to cut off an activity where she was showing a tiny bud of success. A tendon cut on a drinking glass served to effectively stop her practicing the piano just when she seemed to be doing very well. A broken collarbone while water skiing robbed her of a summer's healthy sport. A running bout with pneumonia cut off her budding career as an employment counselor. And a dislocated hip from skylarking around a swimming pool—all within less than a year! She is a classic case of the "accident prone." Many people have tried to reach her, but to no avail. She admits to "masochistic tendencies" but *won't accept the possibility of eliminating this proneness through the PCP energy.* I lost track of her recently, but the last time I heard about her she was still going on from accident to illness to accident. It's a depressing story, and so needless!

This whole book is designed to help you remold your personality and attitudes to Cosmic standards, and in the process eliminate those negative thought areas that used to make us accident prone. But you should also undertake a specific, positive program to root out any remaining traces of accident-attracting tendencies or being prone to accidents beyond control. Let's approach this project from the Taoist ideas of Yang and Yin, or light and darkness. Light is positive and active, while darkness is negative and passive. We are told that darkness is actually nothing of itself, it is only the condition of the absence of light. Similarly we can visualize the life-giving principle as *light,* and the "life-destroying principle" as merely the absence of light, or darkness. Thus we are led again to the conclusion that accident or illness is not a cause in itself, but merely the result of absence of the life giving light in and through the sufferer.

There are both an allegorical and a real light involved in the protection we seek to build. The allegorical light is the light of understanding, and the real light is the life force manifesting as the light-magnetic-substance of your aura. By the regular use of your mind in scientific prayer, in conjunction with sound such as the mystic mantra; you can build a protective wall of living light around your person and your important possessions. Again we are saying that PCP will accomplish anything you are smart enough to ask of it. And certainly divine protection is a proper request!

How to lead a charmed life

We all know a few people who seem to lead "charmed lives." In the past we have called them lucky, or commented "the Lord takes care of fools and drunks"; but now we see that they are working with the Cosmic laws of protection—unconsciously perhaps, but they are working them nevertheless! Start using these wonderful laws to protect yourself and your loved ones, now!

The best method is to visualize a full inch of spiritual armor plate surrounding and protecting you, your loved ones, your motor vehicles, your home, and anything else that is important to your well being. This armor plate is the *living light* of the universal life-giving force, and it is yours for as long as you choose to claim it. Upon arising each morning, visualize your armor plate shining brightly. Then polish it by intoning the mystic mantra a few times while you mentally claim the strengthening and renewing of your PCP protection. And any time during the day when you feel the need of protection, mentally renew it again by repeating the mantra. Learn to *feel* the comfort of the protective power around you always, and enjoy the deep feeling of security that accompanies it. Regularly renew your protection again at bedtime so you go to sleep while basking in the warmth and comfort of the "everlasting arms." Some of you may scoff, but the ones who *use* this simple protective formula will know the living meaning of the Psalmist's exclamation: *Thou shalt not be afraid for the terror by night; nor for the arrow that flieth by day; nor for the pestilence that walketh in darkness; nor for the destruction that wasteth at noonday. A thousand shall fall at thy side, and ten*

thousand at thy right hand; but it shall not come nigh thee.
(Psalm 91:5–7.)

Try it now, and live in the happy light of PCP protection
from this day forward.

Insure your own good health by sharing your PCP

PCP is rather like a muscle. It must be exercised regularly to
keep it in shape. It's important to share the healing PCP
energies regularly. The more we use it, the greater becomes
our capacity to handle it and thus the greater becomes our
apparent supply. We are truly tapping an infinite resource. The
only limitation is the degree of development of our capacity to
direct its tremendous power.

The great rushing stream of PCP energy is flowing easily
within your reach. Shall you dip into it with a thimble, or a
bucket? Or wouldn't it be better to build a pipeline to bring
really big help into your life? The only reason to build a PCP
pipeline is because you *need it.* Need it because you regularly
use it for the good of those around you and for the advancement of mankind in general, and it must and will be yours.

An excellent way to build your PCP pipeline is to use this
wonderful energy twice each day to broadcast healing help to
all mankind. Spend the time! It's much more than just worth it!
Sit comfortably and tune in on the PCP energy. Intone the
mantra, *Om, mane padme, hum,* and feel the power surging
through your being. Then lift your hands and hold them palms
forward as if giving the benediction: and say aloud with a
voice of authority:

**I direct the infinite Psycho-Cosmic Power to flow forth from
me now to touch, heal and bless all mankind and every creature in the universe. It flows forth in waves of healing energy,
sweeping away everything unlike the perfection of the uni-**

versal life force, and replacing it with perfect health, freedom, beauty, and the pure joy of living. I give thanks that it is so now.

Then relax and go about your business in the secure knowledge that *the same PCP energy you so willingly share is protecting you at all times.* Thank the Psycho-Cosmic Power regularly and rejoice in your perfect protection which is now a law of the universe.

Testimonies in proof of PCP healings

In our work through E.S.P. Laboratory we teach our students to visualize the PCP energy as a *healing light.* Here are just a few simple reports from people who have sought help from this *living light.*

A gentleman from New York wrote:

> Since tuning in on your *light* daily, in spite of the fact that I have lost weight, I experienced a feeling of well-being. I am walking fairly well considering the fact that I wear an artificial limb. Several months ago I had great difficulty to read with glasses—today I can at least read in comfort. Also the circulation in my good leg seems to have improved somewhat. . . . I expect to be healed by divine Cosmic spirit, and this will all come to pass for which I am very grateful and thankful.

From a lady in Nevada:

> I am feeling better since you put me on your healing list, and my husband is too. When I wrote you in March I had been ill since November—had X-rays and tests of all kinds. Then in February I got the flu bug and for almost two months pleurisy. In just a few days after using the *healing light,* no more pleurisy pain!

And here is a fascinating discourse on the power of the mind and PCP both to harm and to heal. It comes from a lady in Fresno, Calif.

> I must write you this letter because it is rather unbelievable, also to thank you. First I must tell you I am never sick. I just don't like being sick and haven't been to a doctor for 13 years since my last baby was born. Last month a very dear friend of mine went through a terrible experience. Her daughter-in-law killed one of her children. I went over to help her with the other children and the sight of these neglected children—one beaten until he is mentally retarded and crippled, one so withdrawn she does not want you to touch her—I was so upset for the first time in a long time! I forgot the rules. I condemned the mother, cursed the God that could allow such a thing, and became sick all over. Yesterday I couldn't move a muscle. Every inch of my body was sore and I couldn't stand the touch of clothing. I couldn't lay down, I couldn't sit up, and when I would try to walk, I was so shaky I had to hold on the wall for support. This morning was no better. I got up and tried to work but could do little. I lay down on the bed and prayed for the *healing light* to surround me to heal my mind and my body. I asked forgiveness and in about 30 minutes my mind became clear as a bell, and my body did not hurt any more. I felt strong, well and happy, also very hungry. I hadn't been eating lately. Thank you for your *healing light* and your help.

Points to Remember from This Chapter

1. No disease or condition is absolutely incurable.

2. Pain is one of nature's greatest blessings, it warns us when some part of the body needs help.

3. Jesus demonstrated the art of healing by prayer and the laying on of hands, and challenged us to do likewise.

4. The vital Cosmic life force strives to express itself through you as ever-increasing health, vitality, and effectiveness.

5. Use your PCP energy to heal yourself and others.

6. Build a full inch of Cosmic protective light like spiritual armor plate around your body, your car, your home, and other important possessions. You will never become accident-prone.

7. Build a PCP pipeline based on the need you create when you regularly share it with others.

how to
Let PCP Add a New Dimension to Your Life

In his *Song of Myself*, the great mystic-humanist poet, Walt Whitman, sets the theme for our next considerations. With words of majesty and awe, he implants the firm conviction that a man is certainly not contained between his hat and his shoes. A better understanding of the part of you that is not enclosed within your physical body will add a whole new dimension to your life. Let's carefully consider the following.

A deep Cosmic look at what you are

Modern psychology has a "holy trinity" of its own. Some will immediately think of Freud, Adler, and Jung; but we are thinking here of the *subconscious, conscious,* and *supercon-scious* minds.

The *subconscious* mind is considered to be the seat of the animal instincts and animal emotions, and the controller of the "unconscious" bodily activities such as digestion, heart beat, and cell growth. When its natural desires and drives are repressed or denied reasonable expression, the result is some degree of psychological imbalance.

The conscious mind is the mediator of the "trinity" and

controls our general thinking, reasoning mechanism. It is responsible for directing the external activities of our bodies, and for the "programming" of the subconscious by the quality of the ideas it habitually harbors.

The *superconscious* mind is the seat of inspiration, idealism, morality, and conscience. We might roughly relate the subconscious to Freud's *id,* and the conscious to the *ego.* The superconscious is our personal source of contact with Deity or at least the highest moral and spiritual concepts of the race.

It is important to understand that these ideas of *separate* minds are set out for the purpose of analysis and study. They are generally considered to be aspects of the *one* mind which is the *total consciousness* of the entity. In other words, you are a whole being with many complex aspects.

We might be amazed at the frequency with which some sort of trinity crops up in man's consideration of his own "being-ness." Most occultists and mystics think in terms of a trinity of physical, astral (or emotional), and mental "bodies." There are literally hundreds of sects which somehow weave a threefold nature into the entity called man. One very interesting sect is the Kahuna religion of the Hawaiian Islands. Their concept is simple enough to grasp easily—you consist of a low self, a middle self, and a high self. The thing you most frequently think of as "me" is what the Kahuna calls his middle self, and the psychologist calls the conscious mind. But to the Kahuna, there is a greater separation and autonomy for each of the three "selves," more nearly as if you were three complete beings in cooperative association for your mutual evolution. Thus the low self would be a potentially good and faithful servant, ready to work diligently for the good of the whole entity, but only when properly controlled or guided. And the high self would be seen as a being so far in advance of the middle self as to stand virtually in the relation of a god. The relationship of the Kahuna low self to the subconscious and high self to the superconscious of the psychologist is more than obvious. A slight bridging of the gap from modern psychology to Kahuna thinking will prove very useful to us in understanding our part in the great evolutionary processes of the universe. Thus we will find the means of orienting our personal being into more nearly perfect cooperation and compatibility with the whole of our environment. There is an evolutionary driving force which permeates and directs the whole of creation from the tiniest atom to the vastest galaxy, and we can be comfortable only so long as we obey its laws and respond to its impulses. In effect we must become partners with the universal life force in our own evolution and that of the cosmos.

The evolution of yourself

Psychology concerns itself with "self-actualization," or the comfortable relationship between you and your environment. In the broad field of metaphysics, the same basic idea is expressed as becoming the *actor* instead of merely a *reactor*. The Kahuna puts a little more emphasis on the dynamics of growth, and sets forth the same concept as the *evolution of the selves*. Here the low self is striving to become a middle self, the middle self grows toward becoming a high self, and the high self is evolving toward a state of inexplicable bliss and oneness with the Creator. Each "self" is inextricably bound up in the growth and problems of the other selves which collectively make up the whole entity, just as the entity is bound up in the evolutionary problems of the family, the community, and finally the whole species.

Kahuna teaches that without self-knowledge, man struggles against himself at every turn; producing chaos where there should be harmony, and decadence where there should be only new growth. But isn't this what the psychiatrist means when he speaks of neurosis or psychosis? The Hermetic injunction,

"Man, know thyself," is clearly as useful in our modern society as it was in the time of the ancient civilizations. We will find it enlightening to pursue the Kahuna ideas a bit farther because their clarity and simplicity can take us to a much deeper understanding of the inner workings of the entity called *you*. The key concept is simply evolution—natural development of the whole being through coordinated growth and progress of the three separate selves.

Obviously the three selves can grow only by learning to help each other. But how can we teach them to cooperate? We can get an excellent clue from a glance at our normal social relations with other people. The great secret of human cooperation is *communication*. If you don't understand what your neighbor is trying to accomplish, you can't be of much assistance. But that is exactly the situation which most of us find between our "three selves." The ultimate in good communication is *rapport*. I paused here to see what my dictionary had to say about that word, and it's worth quoting: "In an intimate or harmonious relation; harmony, accord, affinity." From my own experience of rapport, I prefer to call it such a closeness of relationship that feelings and ideas are transmitted or exchanged by people without the necessity or hindrance of normal conversation.

Good rapport is often best demonstrated in a happy marriage. My wife and I enjoy a rapport that is almost startling in some of its manifestations. For instance: we will spontaneously get the urge to go out to dinner somewhere—then we will independently dress, get in the car and drive there; each knowing that the other is in accord without ever bothering to exchange words about it. When you achieve this type of rapport between your low, middle and high selves, you are well on the path to progress and happiness beyond your wildest flights of fancy. Let's take the first steps toward this intra-entity harmony now.

How to communicate with your deeper Cosmic self

Let's start with a brief example of the practical value of communication between the middle self you know as "me," and its low self. A friend who studied Kahuna told me this story:

> A few weeks ago I made a short stop in San Jose on business. I remembered that an old friend and fellow student lived in the town, and I wanted to see her for a few minutes. I talked the situation over with my low self on the way into town, and told it to find her for me. In the rush of the city traffic, I forgot about this for a while. Suddenly there was a small traffic tieup, and I happened to glance into the car stopped beside me. Sure enough, it was my old friend. We stopped for coffee and a friendly chat.

Coincidence? The skeptic would say so. But how many of these "coincidences" do you have to experience before you admit there is much more to it than that?

How to establish rapport with your low self

We will begin building our intra-entity rapport by establishing elementary communications with your *low self*. This low self can be very useful in your daily existence. It can act as your faithful servant, happily running errands and helping you in many ways. Since it is related to the subconscious realms, it has access to the collective knowledge and experience of the human species; and it will gladly share this treasure with another part of itself.

Let's work on establishing the communications system. Your low self is bound to answer your summons, but the degree of its cooperation in your endeavors will be directly related to the understanding and rapport you create by striving for mutuality of purpose for your whole being. Find a quiet place, relax, and call your low self. Say aloud the following words:

I urgently request the presence of my low self for a conference on mutual assistance and cooperation. Please join me now.

Repeat your request firmly and with the *expectation* that you will receive a response. In the beginning, the answer will probably be very subtle, and you will tend to shrug it off as your imagination. But, it would be better to begin in the *imaginary presence* of your low self than not to begin at all! This is the time when an act of faith, that may seem a bit ridiculous to your objective mind, is the stepping stone to greater control of your life activities.

How to assign a name for your low self

First, ask your low self what name you shall use for him. (I use the masculine pronoun for my low self because I am a male; a woman would naturally have a female low self.) One man reached the understanding that his low self had been pretty well running his life, so he gave it the first name he had been using, and began to think of "himself" as a new character. Thus he assumed the use of his middle name for "himself," leaving his first name to the low self.

The new insight and understanding that resulted in this reshuffling of names corresponds to the new name for Jacob after he wrestled with the angel, or the idea of being "born again" expressed by the Master Jesus. It is really similar to a new birth when we learn to control our instinctual self and polarize in the new point of balance we call the middle self.

How to converse with your low self

Let's get back to the conversation with your low self. For the purpose of discussion we will assume you have agreed to call your low self Charlie. Express your thoughts aloud, and address Charlie just as you would another being in a physical body. Your discussion might go like this:

Charlie, it's high time we sat down together to find ways of greater cooperation and mutual assistance in our common goal of evolution. I seek a better understanding of your thoughts and desires so I can blend better with you, and I expect a greater degree of help and cooperation from you.

Your Charlie is very like an adolescent child (and just as real). He needs numerous opportunities to express his individuality and to grow, but he also needs a great deal of guidance and direction. A prerequisite to good relations with your low self is mutual respect. You are striving to train and guide Charlie just as if he were your teenage child. Be generous with your praise for tasks well done, but firm in your directions. Give clear, unambiguous, and non-contradictory orders; and *expect* faithful obedience. You will develop mutual confidence by starting with simple assignments for Charlie. Understand the way he works and reacts, and listen for his explanations and requests.

For instance: You are about to start reading a good book, but you need to make an important telephone call in about an hour. Call Charlie and tell him, "Charlie, I'm about to become absorbed in this book, but I will need to make a phone call. Please call me at exactly three o'clock." Then dive into your book, knowing that Charlie will call you at the right time. At three o'clock, when you get the sudden and strong urge to head for the telephone, be sure to thank Charlie and praise him for his reliability.

How to use the concept of low self

Any metaphysician will recognize that personalizing your concept of the subconscious serves as a strong focal point for the PCP energies. I can accept Charlie as being just as real as my physical body, and a very willing helper along the pathway of personal evolution. If you find this hard to swallow, just think of Charlie as a convenient abstract concept for centering your thought-energy. Either way, *use the concept;* it's the easy way to control your instincts and desires for the good of the whole being of you.

Several people have used their Charlie to cut down or stop smoking. One told him of the decision to cut way down on smoking and asked he be limited to one cigarette per hour. He asked Charlie to make any cigarette lit within less than an hour of the previous one taste so bad he would automatically put it out. It has worked for several years without the habit ever getting the upper hand. With simple techniques like this you can moderate your pleasures without going through the suffering of total abstinence.

If you have a weight problem, you can program Charlie to help you. Tell him to regulate your appetite to enjoy the foods your body needs, but to control your eating so that you will lose one pound each week until you reach a preselected ideal weight, and then hold it there indefinitely. It can be fun to cooperate in joint health efforts with Charlie—now when someone tempts you with that extra piece of pie, you can laugh and say, "No thanks, Charlie won't let me." Charlie can adjust control, and heal any bodily or psychiatric condition, as well as "running errands" that would be impossible for your objective personality to accomplish alone. Work with him and gain his cooperation, but pay attention to his fears and needs as well.

One friend who enjoyed several physically dangerous hobbies confessed to me that he was rapidly giving them up. His Charlie expressed a deep-seated fear of losing the physical body through these activities. "He" complained that he had very recently been deprived of his last physical body in just such activities, and begged for extreme caution or some new outlets for the hobby energy. By making some concessions to assuage his Charlie's fears, this man quickly became a much better functioning entity and received relaxed and effective cooperation from his more comfortable low self. Charlie is an individual, and your understanding treatment of him as such will take you a long way toward becoming a well integrated entity. Why not give it a try?

How to communicate with your higher Cosmic self

When you are polarized in the normal state as your middle self, you stand in the same relation to the higher self as your low self does to you. The high self wants and needs the same cooperation from you that you need from Charlie. Contemplate the tremendous possibilities of this perfect integration. Imagine all three selves in harmonious communication and striving together for the advancement of the whole being. With the inspiration and spiritual power of the high self guiding, the middle self working for growth and improvement, and the low self doing the leg work, the *whole of you* will grow from effectiveness to invincibility.

The best approach to your high self is the respectful attitude you might adopt when seeking advice or help from a relative or trusted friend. Talk over your problems whenever you have a few moments alone. What form will the high self's answer take? This is a little tougher, because your method of communication with your high self may turn out to be completely different from anything I could suggest here. Some people just "get an answer"—they suddenly know, and they know they know, but they can't explain how. Others may see a luminous form before them, or symbols outlined in light, or they may hear a voice. We will go into more detail on means of communication in our next section. Let's close this discussion with the thought that nothing is more important to your over-all advancement than to establish such a sound rapport with your high and low selves that you can completely rely on the results.

When most students reach this point of reliable rapport throughout the entity, they find an immediate turning point that leads them to a wonderously richer and fuller life. Your chronological age doesn't hamper or limit your new happiness and usefulness one little bit. Walter Russell changed his vocation at many different ages, and names like Grandma Moses or Alan Sherman give us the promise that a new career can come as long as breath remains in our bodies. Integrate your three selves into one smoothly functioning entity, and thus open the door to a completely new and wonderful life.

How to use ESP to communicate with your high and low selves

Since effective communication between the three selves that combine to make one *you* is the most important single accomplishment for a human being, we will find it advantageous to take a closer look at possible methods. The middle self we have called the *polarized you* is objective in its normal thinking, reasoning, and perceiving nature. It receives the second-by-second testimony of the external senses or sight, hearing, touch, taste, and smell; analyzes and classifies their apparent meanings, and acts or reacts accordingly. Heretofore this has seemed enough for us, but now we realize we have been using only one third of our basic capability, and we have used even that inefficiently.

We are facing a new problem in communication. Neither the low nor the high self is objective; thus we have a situation analogous to a language barrier. A local businessman received an inquiry from a French concern. The letter was written in French, and it might just as well have been in invisible ink as far as the local people were concerned. They found a professor of French at a local college and arranged for a translation. Then they answered with a letter written in English which no doubt confused the French inquirer as much as the first letter confused the Americans. If you want to be sure of effective communications with another, you must find a common language—even the business and scientific machines of this era are geared to communicate with each other through common language tape or electromagnetic inputs.

What might be the common language of our three selves? Since at least two of them are non-objective, aren't we logically led to some form of extra-sensory-perception? We have been taught to believe that our world consists of three space and one time dimensions. But the only *reality* that we experience is the world of ideas. Now an idea is certainly not an objective thing. You can't hold an idea in your hand for even an instant! We may bring an idea into physical manifestation by means of a material model which will represent our thought. But the thought itself remains forever an intangible something, not explainable by any objective science of today.

But that intangible world contains two of our selves. The low self lives in the world of instinct-experience and race ideas, and the high self lives in the light of inspiration and idealism. They are only approachable through our natural intuition or some developed faculty of ESP. Since this channel of communication is so vital to the integration of the trinity which is you, we will devote our next chapter to the use of PCP to develop an extra sensory channel to use in contacting your non-objective beingness.

Points to Remember from This Chapter

1. Modern psychology looks upon an individual as a "trinity" of subconscious, conscious, and super conscious minds.

2. The mystic Kahuna version of the same "trinity" is your low, middle and high selves.

3. Self actualization, or a comfortable but effective relationship with your environment, is attainable by establishing rapport between the "members" of your trinity of minds.

4. True effectiveness comes from integration of your "three selves" into a smooth functioning unit.

5. You may talk to your low and high selves like you would talk to another human being.

6. The most reliable communication with your "other" selves is logically through the channel of extra-sensory-perception.

how to

Enhance Your PCP Effectiveness Through Extra-Sensory-Perception

Certainly, integration of your total being would be enough reason to develop your extra-sensory-perception. But there are also concrete side benefits of equal importance. Greater knowledge, inspiration and effectiveness await the application of your Psycho-Cosmic Power to the task of opening your psychic faculties.

How to use PCP to develop extra-sensory-perception

We have reached a natural stage in the evolution of the species where individual specimens are beginning to rediscover the extra-sensory powers that were lost to mankind with the development of objective or material intelligence. It was inevitable that the psychic powers of our ancient natures should be pushed into the background by the tremendous expansion of objective material intellect and its scientific reliance on the evidence of the physical senses. But this is no reason for you to

131

fail in the next step of evolution of the human race. Do your part with Cosmic Intelligence—*develop your ESP!*

Workers in the field of parapsychology have related extra-sensory powers to the "normal," objective senses. Thus the extension of sight is called *clairvoyance,* the extension of hearing, *clairaudience,* and the extension of feeling is called *clairsentience.* With the proper application of PCP, *you will find that clairvoyance, clairaudience, and clairsentience are yours almost for the asking!* As with so many things in life, the limiting factor is our acceptance of conditions as they seem in a physical sense. We have been taught since birth to accept the limitations of the five senses, so we go along using only a fraction of our potential. When we wake up to the fact that there is more, we have gained the power to do something about it.

How to contact your important psychic centers

Let's begin with a simple exercise to develop your extra-sensory faculties. For those who want more background on this subject, the theory behind this exercise is explained in my last book, *Helping Yourself with E.S.P.* But here we will concern ourselves with your seven most important psychic centers:

1. The *root center,* located at the base of the spine.
2. The *spleen center,* located along the spine in the area of the spleen.
3. The *solar plexus center,* located behind the navel in the physical solar plexus.
4. The *heart center,* located in the area of the physical heart.
5. The *throat center,* located in the region of the thyroid gland.
6. The *brow center,* located behind and slightly above the eyes, in the region of the pituitary gland.

7. The *crown center*, located near the top of the head, in the region of the pineal gland.

You will be able to pinpoint the location of these centers in your own body by their response to the energies we use in the exercise. Let's try it. Sit or stretch out comfortably where you will not be disturbed. Relax your body and quiet your mind as much as reasonably possible. Begin by making your attunement with the PCP energy. Intone the mystic mantra, *Om, mane padme, hum,* and feel the universal energy flowing into your Cosmic being. Now concentrate on your *root center*. Try to imagine that all of your consciousness exists at that point on the base of your spine. Collect all your thought, feeling and sensation at that one point, and feel the Psycho-Cosmic Power energizing and activating the center. Soon you will feel warmth or a tingling in your root center. As you feel this psychic response, imagine a whirling circle of flame ever growing within the center and increasing its speed and rotation while amplifying the power of the center.

Now direct this same energy to your *spleen center*, causing it to tingle and itself become a vortex of whirling psychic flame. Transfer all your attention to the spleen center, and imagine the flame growing and rotating faster and faster. Feel the PCP energy increasing the power flowing through this center! Then direct the energy to your *solar plexus center* and repeat the whole process there. Intensify the flame and lift it, repeating all the steps, in turn to the *heart, throat, brow,* and finally the *crown* center. When you have your crown center tingling with all the energy you can bring to it, make a statement as follows:

I seek to promote the growth of my whole being by using PCP to stimulate my psychic senses. This is good for me, and I know that my low and high selves are cooperating in every way. I sit in the silence awaiting the voice of my inner self.

Then remain quiet for a few minutes. You may receive no apparent response, or you may be amazed at the immediate results. Either way, you can be sure you are progressing! Continue the exercise daily if possible, but at least three times a week. You will experience an ever-increasing psychic sensitivity which can be put to practical use in many ways. What shall you do with it?

First steps in communication sensitivity

Let's begin by giving our high and low selves a chance to communicate with us. In the quiet moment after you have completed the psychic development exercise, your other selves will naturally work to establish a channel of communication. Most people receive their first contacts by clairsentience or simple intuitive impressions. You somehow feel or sense a presence, or perhaps a new idea. *There will be a good deal of interference from your reasoning mind during this period.* It will tend to belittle or shrug off the weak impressions that first reach you. Be on guard to prevent this interference. By giving attention to these first tiny impressions, we exercise our receiving apparatus and encourage the sending agencies. And thus we grow!

The faculty of clairvoyance most often develops next. With your eyes closed you will begin to notice vague, cloudy pictures or symbols more or less floating by, or changing like a child's kaleidoscope. Here again it would be easy to shrug this off as imagination or changes in the external light, or even as changing pressure on the eyeballs. But your interest and attention will turn this symbolic gibberish into meaningful and valuable communications from the subconscious and superconscious realms. Let your imagination give definite shape to the symbols, then meditate on their possible significance as messages from the other parts of your being.

If a particular symbol puzzles you, ask for an interpretation.

Asking aloud helps to focus your energy and attention. *Expect an answer.* It may come as a simple clairsentient or intuitive impression, or you may see your first signs of developing clairaudience by "hearing" or sensing a voice giving a few words of explanation.

Clairaudience may manifest as a whispered word in your ear at any time. My first introduction was a voice whispering my name in my ear at a time when I was completely alone. It can be quite unnerving if something like this happens when you don't understand it.

Don't be disappointed if you get partial contacts and garbled messages during your development stages. Be thankful for the tiniest manifestation, and work to continually improve your receiving apparatus and channels of communication. These faculties have gone unused for all the years of this life, so it may take some time and a reasonable amount of effort to awaken them. *But ESP faculties can be awakened by any human being at any age!* I can say this because I had to start from scratch to develop my own. In the beginning I believed that I couldn't even see mental images. But perseverance made it develop! Permit me a couple of personal examples taken from our research files. These are questions asked by people who are participating in our psychic research program:

> *Question:* I would like your help to locate my husband's missing wrist watch. He would take it off and put it in a stein on the hutch in the dining room. We have looked all through the house, but can not find it.
>
> *Answer:* I don't feel that your husband's watch has been lost or stolen. Rather, I want to keep looking for it right in the house. I want to go to a place where the dishes are standing up on their edges, rather than lying down, and keep taking all the dishes out of their places until I find it. I see an image of the watch behind one of those dishes.

Response: I want to thank you very much for your help. We found the watch where you said it would be.

    ❀   ❀   ❀

Question: Will I receive a job offer from either White Sands Missile Range, or the Manned Space-craft Center in Houston?

Answer: I saw an image of a bunch of Indian masks floating in the air. Because I have been to White Sands and know there are many Indians in the vicinity, I would take this to be a vote for the White Sands area.

Response: Your Indian masks were an accurate symbol. I got the job in the area you mentioned.

It's never too early or too late. You certainly can't develop ESP yesterday, and you only hurt yourself by putting it off until tomorrow. Start now! Use the psychic development training regularly, and give your subconscious and superconscious selves daily opportunities to contact you.

Practical advantages of communication with your other selves

This is my third book on these psychic subjects, and I already have a publication contract for the fourth. There are many fascinating research activities also taking place under my direction. Many people ask me what all this has to do with being a Certified Public Accountant, which is the profession I was trained for and the way I make a very good living. I am obviously much happier and better adjusted because of the psychic and spiritual work I am now doing. It all started as a result of communication just like we have been discussing.

At an early stage of meditation and seeking of spiritual growth, I received a psychic symbol of an old-fashioned quill pen writing feverishly on a piece of parchment. It was telling me that something inside wanted to write—to share with my fellow man the knowledge that was to come to me. It hasn't come easily, and I was often frustrated with my beginning efforts. But regular guidance and help kept coming, growing stronger as I tried to cooperate with it. It has brought me happiness, health, and a meaning to life that I had no dream of achieving before those early contacts. This is not a special or isolated story with a carefully tailored happy ending. People in all walks of life are led to solutions to problems and to successes that are nothing short of miraculous.

How a leg amputation was avoided

While in terrible pain in the hospital, a man was asked to give permission for the amputation of his leg in order to save his life. He asked for an hour to make up his mind, and when he was left alone he asked for guidance from his low self in its capacity of keeper of the body. He closed his eyes and soon received a clear picture of a figure which looked like him, only many years older. And the figure was walking on *two good legs!* He accepted the promise from his low self, and cooperated with scientific prayer for his healing. More than twenty years later, he is still in excellent health and still walking on *both legs.* He regularly consults his low self on all matters of health, of that you can be sure.

How a legal case was resolved with PCP

A businessman was involved in a lengthy legal battle that increased in bitterness with the passing of time. As is the case with so many of us, his studies of the nature of life and our relationship to the Cosmic had not quite grown into a working philosophy applicable to "real life" situations. But his frustration level was now at the danger point, so he decided to seek help from his high self. He sat quietly and made his mystic attunement with the PCP energies while calling on his high self for guidance. He waited for his answer, but there seemed to be no response. After ten minutes of waiting, he got up in disgust. Just as he started to walk out of the room, an idea "popped" into his head. It was a simple equitable solution with every chance of satisfying all parties to the action. He returned to his quiet place, renewed his attunement, and directed the omnipotent PCP energies to assist in bringing about this solution that would obviously bring the highest good to all concerned. Thus a miserable situation was resolved, leaving pleasant memories instead of the taste of bitterness.

How you can travel outside your physical body

The personalization of the three aspects of self also helps us understand the phenomenon variously known as *astral travel, soul flight,* or *bilocaton.* Under the proper conditions, the part of your being which contains your reasoning consciousness can travel away from and exist apart from your physical body. Let's begin by relating this experience to the familiar process of dreaming.

Some dreams are in color, while others are in black and white; some are jumbled masses of vague symbology, while others are clear and coherent; some are faintly remembered if at all, while others are vivid and seem more real than our morning cup of coffee. Actually those "dreams" which are coherent, and in "living color" are often more than just dreams; and are in fact a form of what we will call an *out-of-the-body experience.* After the first time you leave your body while fully conscious, you will be sure which of your "dreams" are real, and which are fancied.

First steps in astral travel

We will reach an intelligent understanding of the process by learning to duplicate it "on purpose." The preparations are simple, but important. First you must prepare a place to leave your physical body where it will be safe and undisturbed. Your low self, as the guardian of the physical vehicle, will not permit you to leave your body in danger. Your own bedroom is best, particularly if it can be locked from the inside. If your chosen sanctuary isn't equipped with a lock, a ten cent "hook and eye" setup will suffice, and it can be installed with no special equipment in just a few minutes.

Pick a place you would like to visit while out of your body. The more intense your desire, the easier you will find the process of leaving your body, but anxiety will effectively block your exit. So avoid any undue excitement or anxiety.

Now you have retired to the sanctuary of your locked bedroom. Stretch out on the bed and relax. Begin by making the attunement with the Psycho-Cosmic Power. Use the mystic mantra until you feel the energy flowing freely through your whole being. Then call your low self and ask it to stand guard over your body while you are gone. It will help to give the low self a brief explanation that you are seeking spiritual growth by learning the art of projection. When you feel ready, fix your gaze on a spot on the ceiling directly over your head. Imagine that you are looking down on your body from that spot. Feel your consciousness floating upward and slowly collecting right at that spot on the ceiling. Now you are out! Glance back down at your body, then will yourself to travel to your objective. Observe the surroundings you experience so you can later verify that your trip was not merely in your imagination. When you are ready to return to your body, desire it and you will pop back.

It's better to restrict your astral travels to short trips in the beginning. Further along we will add another dimension to this most interesting of human activities, but for the present let's concentrate on acquiring the ability to get out of the body. Don't become discouraged if your first attempts result in nothing more than boredom or falling asleep. The ultimate value of acquiring this ability is worth many hours and weeks of practice and striving. The key is perfect attunement with the PCP energy, combined with perfect relaxation. Keep trying until you succeed!

Some typical first experiences in astral travel

One student described her first experience of leaving the body as follows:

> After a few seconds of the (PCP) "current" I began to feel a definite physical separation. A jolt seemed to be localizing itself in my solar plexus and then started going upward at a higher rate of vibration than before. I think I was leaving with it—also going "upward" away from the solar plexus but I still felt somehow attached to that very spot. I asked then, as you suggested, how I could cooperate. My mind was very alert, more so than usual, and as I was going upward, I realized I was heading for a lighted arena. All at once it was very bright, daylight in fact, and I was on a very busy street in the midst of heavy traffic, cars and buses and people all around me. I was in a big city, seemingly American, but totally unfamiliar. As I know this sometimes happens, I gave an instant thought to my body "back there," and that's exactly where I went—back home to bed. However I was still "with it," because in another moment I was back in the light.
>
> When I looked up, I was alone on a cobblestone street which was right out of Medieval Europe. I have seen this street before . . . only where? . . .

She followed with some interesting descriptive material on several places visited during this experience. I would like to emphasize that this student was fully *awake* at all times during the experience. She experienced two exits and two reentries *all while fully conscious.*

Another good friend and student wrote:

> I came home from work one night around midnight —it had been a very hard drive home as the roads were icy and snow was blowing. I was very nervous when I got in, so I made a cup of hot milk and sat down for a few minutes before preparing for bed. I was *not asleep,* but was more relaxed than I can ever remember being. It stole over me like a soft blanket, and all at once I was standing by a well. I reached to the side and got a dipper and dipped into the well. As I drew the dipper out it was filled with a golden liquid. I poured this over my head and this vapor ran down my body and collected at my feet, and as I looked down, my feet were bare and I felt like I was standing in a cool stream—and then I was again sitting in my chair. I went to bed but could not sleep, so I got up. This vivid manifestation just wouldn't let me go, so I picked up my Bible and just opened it. The verse my eyes fell on went like this: *and I shall remove from your hand the cup of trembling.* I had never seen this verse before. I closed it and now I can't find it again— but I was never fearful of anything anymore. Is it Isaiah?
>
> (Yes, it's Isaiah 51:22.)

As you begin to develop, you may occasionally wake up to discover that you are outside of your body. These are marvelous opportunities to practice controlling your astral activities. Any feeling of fear will cause you to pop right back into your physical body, but that would be a terrible waste. Enjoy some "sight-seeing" before you go back calmly. But most of all, *practice!*

**Now you know you can exist apart from
your physical body**

Your very first out-of-the-body experience will change your
understanding of life forever for the better. Once you have
settled comfortably on the ceiling, looked down on your dor-
mant body, then floated away; you have gained a completely
new insight into that previously theoretical *eternal life* you
have heard preached so often. Since you can exist apart from the
physical body, its so-called "death" would obviously not be the
end of you! Thus the achievement of your first astral flight
gives you *clear title to eternal Cosmic life.* You have had it
always, of course, but now you KNOW you have it, and
nobody can take it away from you. Meditate on this for a
while. It will inspire you to redouble your efforts to achieve
astral projection.

A little contemplation of your new insight into eternal Cosmic life leads to another fascinating conclusion. *If you are
eternal, then all other humans must be eternal also!* Thus we
realize that the wisdom and experience of the ages does not
pass out of existence with the passing of great men of history.
Somewhere the great personalities of yesteryear must be going
about their business of life with all their accumulated knowledge—though living in a dimension as yet unknown to our
scientific world. We only need a way to tap this wonderful
source of wisdom to bring much help to ourselves and mankind.

How to tap the wisdom of the ages

Personalities not living in physical bodies at the present time
are generally referred to as *spirit entities,* or simply *spirits.*
Substantial help can be gained from contact with dwellers in
the spirit dimension of life. Their world and ours are separated

only by a thin veil which is easily bridged with the help of extra-sensory-perception. And spirit entities have the same stake in the evolution of life on our planet as we who are presently manifesting ourselves in *physical bodies.*

There is a wonderfully reciprocal relationship between so called *"physically* living" beings and members of the spirit world. Not only is our path of evolution intertwined with theirs, but their every act of helping us is a means of growth and progression for our spirit friends.

A little reflection will convince you that there are many more souls on the "spirit" side of life than confined on earth in bodies of flesh. Thus we will contact and work with many spirits in the course of fulfilling our period of study in the classroom called earth life. We are each constantly assisted by unseen hands! But think of the improved efficiency if we will simply and knowingly cooperate with this excellent help.

Right now *you* have a band of spirit helpers who work with you more or less exclusively. Their help can be broad and vague, or very specific, depending on your willingness to accept and cooperate with it. They can help you accomplish anything you desire.

How a practical spirit helped a hairdresser

Permit me an example from my experience with a good friend. We went out to dinner with a couple, and during the course of the evening we heard the story of the wife's difficulties in beauty school. As she put it, "My theory is excellent, and I wash, cut and set well; but I just can't seem to comb hair out properly."

We returned to their home, and as we relaxed in the living room, I glanced up and saw a spirit figure outlined in the doorway. We communicated briefly and I happily said to our "living" friend, "There is a spirit entity here who gives me the name of 'Joan.' Joan would like to further her progression by helping you with your comb-outs. When you reach that point next time, just relax and let her work through you."

Toward the end of the following week, I received a nice note from our friend. It said in part:

> I talked to "Joan" all the way to school Monday, and there were no "butterflies" in my stomach when I began to comb out my first patron. That brush and comb moved along just exactly like they knew what they were doing. It was the style I had fought all the prior week. My instructor was so surprised when he made the final check. He didn't have to correct one single hair! And needless to say, my patron was very pleased.

Thousands of people are helped every day by cooperating with their spirit helpers. *You* can be helped too! It's worth a little effort to develop the contact.

Your first simple steps to spirit contact

Let's see how easy spirit contact can be. Perhaps you have already met some of your spirit helpers while on an astral flight, but it isn't necessary to get out of your body to communicate with the other side of life. You can do it in the calmness of your own meditation place. Relax and make your normal PCP attunement. Then call your low self and direct it to invite your spirit helpers to visit you. In a sense, your own low self is a kind of spirit entity. So your methods of communication with the low self will give you the best clue to spirit communication.

This will naturally require the use of ESP, but our prior work has already fitted you for this rewarding undertaking. Your individual spirit friends may inform you of their presence in unique ways that somehow fit their own personalities. Many will show you some kind of symbol clairvoyantly, some may whisper in your ear, others may touch you with an electric vibration or the feeling of a gentle breeze on your cheek. We have one interesting friend who greets us by producing a pungent odor which smells like the burning of oriental herb incense. Logically you should be as polite to your spirit friends as you would be to earthly friends who drop in to see you. Greet each one by name whenever you recognize it! This will help to establish better contact.

Some will ask, "But how shall I know their names?" This also comes through your ESP. When you see each new symbol, or otherwise sense a new presence, ask for the name, and accept the impression that is sent to you. You may have occasional visits from relatives, but your most important contacts will come with those entities who are assigned to work with you in your personal evolution. It is your duty to work, grow, and *achieve.* The Master Jesus taught these things by word and example, and he left us with the great challenge: *These works that I do shall ye do also, and even greater works shall ye do. . . .* It will prove well worth your while to try!

Points to Remember from This Chapter

1. Use the psychic development exercise to unfold your own extra-sensory-perception.

2. Many practical advantages will be yours when your ESP is well developed.

3. You can also use PCP to learn to travel outside of your physical body.

4. Your out of the body experience will prove the certainty of eternal life and the existence of the "spirit world."

5. The wisdom of the ages still lives in the spirit world, waiting for you to tap it.

6. Send your low self to invite your spirit helpers to visit you. Then enjoy the companionship and help.

how to

Use PCP to Become
Socially Successful and
Gain Many New Friends

Sometimes we want to meditate or just sit and think, but
most of the time we require the company of other people to
stimulate us to true enjoyment of life. Our psychologists and
sociologists tell us that man is a gregarious animal—he enjoys
the companionship of his fellow creatures. And we also enjoy
being enjoyed by our fellow beings.

Popularity adds zest to your life

We often hear that an entertainer's spiritual food is the
applause of his audience. Not only is this a true statement, but
there is some degree of the actor or entertainer in each of us. A
certain part of you regularly cries out for the applause and
approval of friends and acquaintances, or even the public in
general. This spiritual food is as important to our well-being as
the material food that nourishes our bodies. Everyone benefits
from the enjoyment of a wide variety of social contacts, the
exchange of ideas, and the general stimulation to personal
growth which results from increasing popularity.

There is another practical reason for widening your circle of friends and acquaintances. Let's put it simply *that it pays to be liked*, which is part of saying it pays to be pleasant and helpful to everyone. Aside from the warm glow of shared pleasures or acts of kindness, you never know when some apparently insignificant person you befriended will be in position to give you some real help—some day. We had a standing bit of scuttlebut (gossip) in the Navy about the Chief Petty Officer who was rotated back to "the States" six months early by a lowly yeoman he had helped out of a bad situation. The Chief had been home several weeks before he found out how he made it. Life's best policy toward your fellow man is to treat each person you meet as if he were about to become the owner of the company which employs you.

How to build your launch pad to ever greater popularity

You walk into a room full of strangers. One of them gives you an icy stare and looks away, while another smiles and says, "Hi, there!" Which one do you warm up to? Now think back to the last time a stranger walked into a room containing you. How did you greet him? (or her?)

Immediately some lovely young lady will say, "I don't dare try that! It would be misinterpreted as too forward or flirting, and get me into too many wrestling matches." But there is no truth to that idea. You can be warm and friendly, and still maintain all necessary dignity and control of any situation. The essence of being a lady or gentleman is the use of your ability to make everyone around you comfortable and at ease. Certainly this must begin with a warm greeting and a friendly smile.

Consider your general attitude and approach to life as you

display it to others. No one enjoys being around a grouch or chronic complainer. Naturally you don't fit this category, but look at yourself objectively for a moment. Are you sure you don't fit there once in a while? There are occasional days when things seem to get started on the wrong foot, and progress to something worse. How do you suppose you look to your fellow beings at the end of a day like that? Can you think of somebody who bears up so well under trying circumstances that his friends call him "smiley" or "laughing boy"? You could do much worse than to earn such a nickname.

As you develop the habit of bringing a positive attitude to all situations, you are putting a firm foundation under your launch pad to popularity and adding a new dimension of comfort to your life at the same time. There is some element of good in even the most terrible or ridiculous situations. Learn to look for it and verbalize it, not as a Pollyanna but as a confident human being. It will work wonders for your disposition as well as your appeal to your fellow humans.

Look upon your new role in life as that of a roving ambassador of goodwill to all mankind. Be constantly alert for opportunities to perform little acts of kindness—a pat on the back or word of encouragement at the right time can be a turning point in someone's day or even his whole life. A cutting remark left unsaid, a door held open for someone with an armload, the right of way yielded to a motorist having trouble entering the stream of traffic—small gestures of goodwill that become part of your moment-by-moment habit-action patterns add a growing sense of personal worth while endearing you to every person you contact. Such a consciousness can be built only by piling up tiny bits of kindness over a period of time until it becomes a solid part of your personality. It will prove to be your most valuable personal asset. Start practicing now! And continue for the balance of this sojourn on earth.

Your steady application of these simple ideas will build the strongest possible launching pad to personal popularity. The only other necessary ingredient is the increase of your personal magnetism.

How to use PCP to increase your personal magnetism

People often talk about personal magnetism but they use the phrase allegorically, not realizing that there really is a magnetic something which attracts people and "lucky breaks" to those who use it properly. In the discussion of the low self I used an example of sending it out to arrange a meeting with a specific person. This will work consistently and effectively, but a note of caution is in order. Use of the low self to cause another person to be inconvenienced is an encroachment on the other's privacy and right to self determination. Exercise of control over another, even something seemingly as harmless as coming to meet you, borders on "black magic" and must be used with extreme care. By willfully exercising our powers without consideration of the rights of others, we produce karmic or cosmic debt situations which will be collected from us by the law of the Cosmic universe at some very possibly inconvenient time. But enough of the cautions. You have a mind which is capable of telling right from wrong—just be sure you use it!

Our primary purpose is not to produce magnetism for the attraction of specific individuals, but rather a generally beneficent force that will strongly attract the goodwill and fine opinions of all the people we meet. The launching pad ideas are of extreme importance to this undertaking because we will be using the PCP energy to amplify the impressions we make on people. The flavor of the impression remains that which we produce by our basic social actions each time we are in the company of another human being. Think this over thoroughly *before* you begin. We are setting out to *amplify* (multiply the power) the psychic impressions and attractions sent from your being to the psychic receptors of your contemporary beings. Therefore it is urgent that you send out only strongly *positive* impressions!

How shall we increase the magnetic power of our Cosmic emanations? Think of your body as the core of a huge magnet. Just as there are naturally magnetic minerals, there is a certain amount of natural magnetism in each of us. But the strongest magnetic fields are produced by the flow of electricity through coils of wire wrapped around in suitable core. Your physical body is your core, the higher body of light takes the place of the coils, and the PCP energy flows under the direction of your will to produce a wonderful improvement in your personality. Sit quietly and use the mantra to bring your PCP attunement to a peak, then direct the energy to flow through your being, increasing the power of your personal magnetism while purifying its radiations. Feel the magnetic power surging through your being and out into the space around you.

Practice directing your magnetic energy to broadcast a silent greeting of goodwill to every person who comes near you. Silent radiation of goodwill has a positive effect on even the most "withdrawn" or coldly aloof people.

How to renew your personal magnetism

You will find it valuable to renew your personal magnetism every morning, as soon after arising as possible. Make it part of your morning ritual to amplify your magnetism and send it as love and goodwill to all mankind. It will help set your mood for the day and color your experience with pleasantness reflected back from your surroundings. An old breakfast food commercial went, "Start your day a little bit better. . . ." The words fit our situation perfectly: *start your day a little bit better by amplifying your magnetism and radiating it as love and goodwill to all mankind.* Then any time you need a lift or help in handling an uncomfortable situation, direct the Psycho-Cosmic Power to increase your personal magnetism and radiate it as goodwill to the people you must encounter. It can be the difference between success and failure in your every undertaking.

How to handle special personalities

We find ourselves in frequent contact with many people who are not particularly "close" to us. These associations will be pleasant or miserable in accordance with the effort we put out to keep them warm, fresh and interesting.

How do you get along with your boss? Your mother-in-law? Your co-workers? Your subordinates? A brief check of your attitude toward each of these will help to improve daily relations with the vast majority of contacts.

Let's look at your boss first! Are you sure you think of him as human? How often do you orient yourself to his thinking by mentally putting yourself in his place? In your mental position as "boss" you now have to get a definite amount of work and effectiveness out of the group of people which includes the *old you.* How do you and your fellows look from this vantage point? Does this help you get a better understanding of his moods and drives? An excellent addition to your morning ritual is to radiate goodwill specifically to your boss as part of sending it to the whole world.

Someone will complain: "But my boss is a complete Scrooge, skinflint and tyrant! Nobody can possibly get along with him!" If you are right, you owe it to yourself to quit, and seek a position with more congenial surroundings. But before you undertake such a drastic solution, try this simple experiment. First promise yourself that you will definitely quit in 90 days if conditions are not materially improved. Then devote the 90 days to radiating goodwill to the man in question. Every time you start to get exasperated, stop and put yourself in his place. Try honestly to see the situation from his point of view, even if you still don't agree with it. Then from your new position of understanding, radiate goodwill where you previously sent only bitterness. Without being too obvious, find little things to say that are complimentary to the boss. Then don't necessarily say them to his face, but be certain to say them behind his back. Make your associates start looking at the good qualities in the man—the qualities that built the business or at least elevated this man to his position of responsibility. If you haven't created a whole new happy relationship with your boss and your job in 90 days, then it really is time to quit.

So on to the next personality! Did you know that *mothers-in-law can be fun?* Probably the most maligned of all human relationships is that of one spouse to the other's mother. But this display of negativity is simply a result of both parties' behaving like belligerent children. It takes only one of you to begin a whole new era of pleasantness. It's easy to be agreeable in her company! When she makes a suggestion, why argue with her? Why not agree at the moment, then later do as you please? Naturally it's best not to give the in-laws a voice in running your homelife, but it isn't necessary to be unpleasant about it either. Where you can "yes" them in person and do as you please later, you will produce the least friction. But when it is necessary to take a stand, be unyieldingly firm with a bright smile on your face. After a little time spent in getting rid of the friction that may remain from the past, you can honestly look forward to occasional visits.

How do your fellow workers feel about you? Do they think of you as a team player? Or a would-be star? Do you feel their opinion is justified? The support and respect of your associates must be earned by honest effort, and by fair treatment of everyone! Leave the petty politics to the small-minded people who revel in it. Backbiting or indulging in malicious gossip may seem like fun, but *you* can't afford the effect on your consciousness or your reputation. Your ever-improving friendly and helpful approach to life will endear you to all your fellow beings if you remember to avoid the little bits of negativity that seem so enticing.

What of your subordinates? Do you treat them like people too? If for no reason other than personal protection, you will find it prudent to be extra considerate of those who spend their working days following your instructions. Who knows where you will meet one of them twenty years from now? You may easily find yourself working for one of them some day. The treatment you may expect then is clearly related to the treatment you are giving now. Don't ever forget it! Then when you wind up owning a vast industrial complex, the consideration you have given everyone along the way will be a real comfort to you in your quiet years of retirement.

How to enjoy close friendships with PCP

Friendships don't just happen! They are the natural product of exposure and compatibility with Cosmic Law. You can sit alone in your living room for the next twenty years and never make one new friend. If you would like more friends, the first requirement is that you take the trouble to meet new people. As always, some of your new acquaintances will be interesting, while others will more or less leave you cold. We will let you decide what to do about the ones who don't turn you on, and concentrate on those with whom you find a measure of compatibility.

When you sense compatibility with a new acquaintance, the natural inclination is to get to know each other better. Here is a happy chance to experience the sheer joy of sharing expression with another being. During the get-acquainted period you will notice some degree of rapport growing between you. In this case we use rapport to mean that you seem to be tuned to the same frequency—you sense each other's thoughts, and tend to want to do the same things at the same time. Mutual attention to the building of rapport will yield some positive results, but the truly remarkable relationships are founded on a natural affinity that was there from the beginning. You will benefit from working to improve your rapport with everyone you know, but the real depths of experience are attainable with only a select few who vibrate to your natural frequency.

How to improve rapport with all people

It takes mutual effort to materially improve any human relationship. But a joint undertaking must be suggested by one individual. Why not let it be you? You might tactfully approach the subject by saying, "John, do you think it would be interesting to experiment with thought transference?" When you get a positive response, arrange some time together where the atmosphere is calm and peaceful. Then try this simple experiment:

One person picks a mental image of some simple object like a lamp, vase, cup, or spoon, etc., and concentrates on sending this image to the mind of the other. The receiving party simply relaxes and closes his eyes to see what may appear on the little mental television screen inside his head. Some receivers will get a feeling, sensation or impression rather than an image; but if the idea is actually transmitted, you know you are making progress. Try it when you first get together. Then enjoy a little joking and small talk for a while to establish a feeling of shared experience. Next try the telepathy experiment again and notice how much easier the mental exchange becomes. This can be a fascinating game as well as an excellent producer of mutual psychic growth.

Once you develop telepathic affinity with someone, you will enjoy sending thoughts over a distance. Pick a time when you can both sit down for the experiment. Let one plan to send for the first five minutes, and then receive for the next five. Each receiver should write down his (or her) impressions. Then you can check by phone, or next time you meet. As the rapport develops, you will find that you are able to send each other simple messages without a prearranged time. Every time you successfully transmit a thought to a friend, you are not only stimulating mutual psychic growth, but you are also contributing to the psychic evolution of all mankind.

There are many benefits of friendship other than the excitement and fun of telepathic communication. It is the nature of man to enjoy the company of other members of his species, but there is always more to it. As you learn to be genuinely interested in the welfare, progress, and happiness of another, you are realizing more of your potential as a true expression of Deity. God lives in and through His creations. So every experience of living in and through a friend brings you closer to the creator of the universe. Enjoy your many friends—it's well worth the effort to keep adding new ones!

Points to Remember from This Chapter

1. Life takes on increased meaning as you become more popular with your fellow beings using PCP.

2. Build your launch pad to popularity by developing your friendly smile and the habit of regular little acts of kindness to everyone you meet.

3. Accept your new role of ambassador of goodwill to all mankind.

4. Use PCP to increase your personal magnetism.

5. Enjoy the depths of friendship by establishing telepathic rapport with someone of mutual affinity.

6. Find yourself closer to Cosmic Good by living in and through the expression for another's good.

how to

Use PCP to Attract and Hold Your Perfect Mate

There are many conflicting clichés on the subject of love and marriage. "Marriages are made in heaven." "Marry in haste, repent at leisure." "Any two normally intelligent people should be able to make a go of marriage."

Let's not be bound by old clichés

From early childhood we were plagued by the idealistic notion that "Marriages are made in heaven." But now we find that most modern ministers have eliminated the phrase, "Until death do us part," from their marriage ceremony. The reason is that they don't want to make so many people into hypocrites. Our free society is based on the unlimited choice of individuals as to when and with whom they shall enter the marriage relationship. It would be obvious foolishness to say that individuals are incapable of making mistakes in other matters of free choice, so let's not be naïve enough to think that the choice of a marriage partner is somehow different. In the heat of infatuation we tend to gloss over all the little annoying traits that may later grow up into huge rifts. Manufacturers still put erasers on pencils, and typewriter correction fluids still sell in

159

tremendous quantities. It's no wonder that our divorce courts are full of miserable people who seek to erase another kind of mistake.

Don't let anybody confuse you with the bit about "any two normally intelligent people should be able to make a go of a marriage." *To tell you how easy it is, these "do-gooders" stress compromise as the key to happiness!* But it is altogether possible that there are areas of a poor relationship where a 50/50 compromise would be completely unpalatable to either party. Compromise may be a way to prolong a poor relationship and keep it from breaking out into total war, but in a marriage based on real affinity and compatibility there is rarely a need for compromise—the two partners naturally want the same things, and long to achieve the same goals by the same methods.

Some may claim that the idea of a marriage with no necessity for compromise is just as idealistic as the concept that all marriages are made in heaven. In one sense this may be correct, but it has one useful difference. It gives us a rough standard to apply to our relationship *before* we wake up across the breakfast table from a total stranger. The premarital period should be a time of careful and reasonably objective study. It's not as important to know everything about your potential partner as to completely understand your reaction to every thought, mood, habit, and mannerism of this about-to-be-spouse. Your PCP can help you to do all this.

Tensions or comfort is the question. That old thing about "The course of true love never runs smooth" is another vicious distortion of the truth. It's true that your love for each other may vary in intensity from time to time, but there is no reason whatever for arguments or fights. That kind of discord indicates that one or probably both parties are emotionally immature and unfit for a deeply romantic relationship. If you feel at all dominated or "pushed" by a potential marriage partner, break off the relationship in a hurry! Life is way too long to spend it in misery and tension.

My own experience in marriage using PCP

My favorite way to explain real, undemanding, but completely lasting love is to relate it to my old sweater. For fifteen or twenty years, I had an old sweater that was my personal symbol of relaxation and pure comfort. I put on the sweater whenever I felt physically down, or needed an emotional lift. It was much like Linus' (of the comic strip *Peanuts*) security blanket, but without the deep seated necessity. It never demanded attention, but was always there any time the symbol of creature comfort was appealing. When I met the girl who is now my wife, the first sensation I remember is that same feeling of comfort I had always associated with the sweater!

The years of happy marriage are beginning to stretch out now, and they are all the more important to us because we had each made mistaken marriages before this one. I threw away my old sweater after the first date with this girl—I didn't need it any more. And as this is written, we can look back and honestly say there has never been tension or strain between us.

It is well worth all the striving and refraining from premature marriage that may be necessary to find the measure of rapport and compatibility that will make your marriage tension-free. But if you are human like the rest of us, you may need spiritual help to find it. Right at the time when we need our clearest thinking, we find ourselves intoxicated with the infatuation people confuse with love, and we are unable to objectively study the budding relationship.

You could use your PCP if only you knew what to use it for! But you are still not alone. This is the time to call on your higher self to bring you guidance from all necessary places.

Spend a great deal of time at your altar (in your own heart) praying for help in recognizing your perfect mate when the happy time of manifestation comes. This is a time when your high degree of attunement with the PCP forces will stand as your protection from error, and a bearer of happiness closely resembling the ideal of perfect marriage. How shall you prepare for this most wonderful of human relationships?

How to build your launch pad to perfect companionship

Contrary to most adolescent dreams of marriage, the key to success is your orientation to *givingness*. Meditate on the joys of giving to your mate—bringing true comfort, inspiration, solace, joy, and *freedom*. Let's pause to consider the emotion we call *love*. It is important to turn loose of our selfish and childish notions about this most important relationship between man and woman. If we are to fulfill our potential as gods, we must certainly be godlike in our loving. When we think of God's love, we are automatically led to the concept of givingness: *For God so loved the world that He gave . . .* And even in the process of giving the world a great teacher like Jesus, God also gave His creatures the freedom to accept or reject both the teacher and His teachings!

We might best think of mature love as a *genuine interest in the welfare and advancement of the love object* that manifests as a constant *desire to give of one's self*, coupled with the *ability to understand when the object of our givingness is not ready to accept or receive*. In other words, we are speaking of *giving with no strings attached*. When you think of love and marriage to a specific individual, do you have any desire to change his (or her) habits or mannerisms, or way of speech or dress? If so, you are certainly *not ready* for marriage! Any desire or intent to control your companion is proof positive that what you think is love is really a sham and a farce. You may be in love with love, or in love with your ideal of what a companion should be. But it is not love of the *person* if you have the slightest desire to superimpose your will on his (or hers).

Now some doubting person may ask, "But if I'm only concerned with *giving* to my companion, how can I keep from being walked all over like a doormat?" The answer is simplicity itself. When you have found your true mate, you will be pleased to find that he (or she) is just as interested in giving to you as you are to him. Thus you establish a relationship based on mutual consideration, instead of the usual tugging and pulling we confuse with connubial bliss. Is this too idealistic to be practical? I honestly don't think so. You will never be comfortable in marriage if you settle for less. And if you feel it necessary to compromise, it's still good to have a clearly formulated ideal for a yardstick. Then at least you'll know what you are trading for the illusion of security or whatever it is you are tempted to sell out for.

PCP will help to clearly define your idea of a perfect marriage and a perfect mate for you. What are the traits and interests you expect to find in your perfect mate? Think of writing a set of specifications for a mate, like you were designing a house or picking out your dream sports car. It's a good idea to follow through with the exercise and actually write out the specs. Then review them from the viewpoint of your new mate, and write the companion set of specifications you might expect him (or her) to have for you. How well do you fit your imaginary partner's specs? This will give you a pretty good idea of the adjustments you need to allow in your own specs if you are to achieve an actual relationship in the practical world. The more honest you can be in this exercise, the better you will be able to know the real thing when it comes along.

We are preparing to use our PCP to attract and marry your perfect mate. But let's take care to lay a good enough groundwork that we succeed in marrying the right person. If you carefully define your ideal and project it into the realms of PCP, you will be forever amazed at the perfection of the result. Even down to the smallest things, my wife and I find ourselves in perfect sympathy of mood and desires. We get tired at the same times, we soar to heights of spiritual ecstasy together, then tenderly nurse each other over life's little rough places. But the thing that makes it all worthwhile is the ever growing bond of *mutual consideration.* And this relationship is never a strain on either of us—simply because we do what we feel, ever knowing that our every action toward one another will be accepted and understood. This isn't just a lucky accident! Our former spouses would undoubtedly testify that we are both hopeless misfits in this world. And we would agree completely. But in a larger sense, we're all misfits. What we need is to find another misfit who is out of step with the world in the same way we are. My wife and I were drawn together not by accident but by carefully directed prayer. We were each using the PCP energies to attract an ideal mate. And it worked perfectly for us, even as it will for you. The law holds no grudges, and is no respecter of persons. It cannot refuse to work for you.

Embark now on a period of prayer and meditation to perfect your ideal of a perfect marriage partner, so we can turn on PCP and bring your perfect result.

How to be ready to attract your perfect mate

We learned the first step in attracting your perfect mate in our last chapter. It is simply to increase your personal magnetism. The attractive force that inevitably brings your mate into your life is nothing less than your own dynamic personal magnetism *amplified by Psycho-Cosmic Power.*

Begin in your quiet place, and make the PCP attunement.

Feel your overwhelming oneness with the universal life force, and direct it to flow through your being and affairs, amplifying your personal magnetism. Then talk to the PCP energy:

Infinite Power of the Universe, I am ready to attract my perfect mate now. I have studied the meaning of the marriage relationship, and understand both its obligations and the growth we will earn together. I direct the Psycho-Cosmic Power to attract my divine companion to me NOW!

Then give your heartfelt thanks for the certain working of the law. But your part in the game doesn't end with the simple pulling of the PCP trigger. It is equally important that you set out to help yourself. Why should you expect the PCP energy to bring your companion to your living room couch all gift wrapped? Get out of your house and go places where you are likely to meet a suitable companion. And always stay alert to the guidance that tells you when you do meet your new partner!

There are many ways this guidance may come to you. I met my wife in a tiny church. She was performing healing by prayer and the laying on of hands. I sat in her healing chair, and when she walked up behind me, I felt a spark radiate from her to me. A tingling sensation, a "funny" feeling, or some extrasensory impression may alert you to this power manifestation. Then you are ready to embark on a wonderful courtship. But a word of caution is in order. We sometimes get overeager for our manifestation and let our imagination run away with us. Test your spirit guidance carefully before you place too much faith or hope in it. Remember, *you and only you are responsible* for your less than careful actions. Know what you are doing *before* you let your emotions carry you away.

How to handle the courtship period

The courtship period is most important because it lays the foundation for the whole marriage relationship. We may find ourselves straining to put our best foot forward, to gloss over the other's glaring shortcomings, and generally to strive for *impression* at the expense of *sincerity*. Perhaps the lack of sincerity is completely unconscious and obscured by anxiety, but it is important to look for it and carefully root it out. The best gift you can give to this budding relationship is to *be yourself*. Relax completely, and put your companion at ease.

Give of your time as freely as possible during this exciting period. Strive to share your hopes and dreams, your ideals and prejudices, and all your attitudes to the important elements of life. Study your companion carefully. It is a good idea to make a written checklist for areas of compatibility and conflict. Even if you don't care to put it on paper, a mental checklist is essential. How do you stack up together on these vital points:

(1) Religion (2) Economic goals (3) Periods of greatest activity (e.g. early riser vs. night owl) (4) Types of hobby and recreational interest (5) Tastes in humor (6) Attitudes toward sex (including the *intensity* of the appetites) (7) Inclination to physical vs. mental activity?

Don't pass any premature judgments in either direction. Balance the ideals of perfectionism with the practical view that you can expect no more from your companion than you can bring to the relationship yourself. Realize that you would be terribly uncomfortable living with a person who is perfect. It isn't perfection in a mate that we must seek! Rather it is the *harmonious blending of your imperfections!* Don't look for the areas of perfection or strength in your companion, but study the imperfections and weaknesses. Can you live with them for the rest of your life and not become more and more "bugged" by them? Find ways to spend a great deal of time together in situations closely resembling the routine of married life to get the feel of the way you will react to each other when the glamour of the courtship has faded away.

How to insure a long-term happy marriage

If you have to "work at it," your marriage was a mistake from the beginning. But even if it was a mistake, all is not lost! The only sure element in life is evolution. Two people embark on a marriage at least close enough together to be deluded that they are headed along the high road to eternal romance. Children's story books end with, "and they got married, and lived happily ever after." But the grown-up world belies the fantasy. For every divorce that actually reaches the courts, there are two or three other homes where the occupants would be greatly relieved to live apart, if only they had the courage to take the giant step. What happens after the preacher says "I now pronounce you man and wife"?

The answer again is evolution. You grow either together or apart. But as intelligent beings, you have control over your direction of growth. Perhaps the greatest single force for the improvement and maintenance of good marital relations is a common religious seeking. The old bromide about the family that prays together stays together is based on very sound reasoning. The part of your being that cries out for union with and experience of Deity is also the part most capable of tender emotions like love and consideration. When a couple unites in striving to develop this "soft" side of their natures, the warm glow of mystical union tends to carry over into their daily attitudes toward each other. Mutual agreement to seek growth in other areas of life; including joint hobbies, recreation, and pursuit of knowledge; will build bridges where none existed before.

It is proper to hold on to your ideas of a perfect marriage. Contemplate all the good parts of your present relationship, and expect them to get better and better. Remember there is never any tension between truly divine companions. It takes two people to generate tension! You can eliminate much if not all of it by the simple decision to quit pushing on your partner. That old law of Physics is equally true in human relations: *To every action there is an equal and opposite reaction.* In other words, every time you push or pull on your partner, there is a natural tendency for a reaction in kind. All this is perfectly understandable using your PCP.

It's logical to assume that you can eliminate half the tension by completely ceasing to put pressure of any kind on your partner. Then by mastering your own reactions you should be able to get rid of even more. If there are uncomfortable tensions in your marriage you are headed for big trouble. Root it out immediately! Give it to your PCP for effortless handling. But what if it seems completely unbearable already? Try this simple experiment: Promise yourself to make a maximum effort to get rid of the marital tensions—that for a period of 60 days you will not only refrain from putting pressure on your spouse, but you will react with warmth, friendliness and consideration to every situation. Give the situation to your Psycho-Cosmic-Power! Then at the end of the 60 days of intensive effort, you will know if comfort is worth the trouble.   If it isn't, then break it up as quickly as possible. Life is far too long to spend it wallowing in tension and misery. *You are entitled to a story-book married life.* It's yours for the claiming! PCP can be used to smooth out the rough spots, or bring the missing ingredients to any marriage, so long as both partners agree on the goals and work together.

Work intelligently to make the dream come true: *live happily ever after.* A happy, affectionate, comfortable marriage leaves you much more energy and drive to apply to the rest of life's challenges. It's one of the major keystones in the framework of a successful life. Start now to make your homelife "perfect" with your divine companion.

Points to Remember from This Chapter

1. In an ideal marriage there is no need for compromise.

2. The real test of the perfect relationship is complete relaxation and comfort in each other's presence.

3. Cosmic love is *givingness* and *freedom*.

4. Write a set of specifications for your perfect mate. Then write the companion's specifications for you. Compare the two and understand where you will have to bend your specifications to make a practical relationship. Then give them to your PCP to develop.

5. Use your PCP to amplify your personal magnetism and attract your perfect mate.

6. Stress sincerity over impression during the critical courtship period. Look for the harmonious blending of your *imperfections*.

7. Insure a happy, long marriage by faithfully using the principles of PCP daily in overcoming marital problems.

how to

Use PCP to Sweep Unwanted People and Conditions Out of Your Life

Let's carry on with the basic idea of freedom from tension we began to unfold in the last chapter. The greatest curse of our modern era is the anxiety and tension born of our failure to control external conditions, or at least adjust to them. A commonly used prayer in self-help circles goes something like this: *God grant me the Serenity to bear the things I cannot change, the courage to change the things I can, and the wisdom to know the difference.* Our Cosmic approach is a little more optimistic! It is simply this: *you can change anything, if you first learn its lesson.* You have all the power you need, it's just a matter of learning to use it.

You are on earth to express the magnificence of Cosmic Deity

With all his scientific and technological progress, man still gazes in awe at demonstrations of nature's titanic forces. Words like *hurricane, earthquake, flood, forest fire,* and *typhoon* still make us uncomfortable if not downright uneasy.

The thought of such tremendous natural power running amuck makes us realize the puniness of our own physical powers and helps us maintain a healthy perspective of our importance in the Cosmic scheme of things.

We contemplate nature's vast powers and feel totally insignificant. But the balancing thought comes form observing a tiny blade of grass stubbornly growing up through three inches of "solid" concrete. What man in his right mind would consider pitting the strength of a tiny blade of grass against a massive block of concrete? Viewed in that manner it doesn't make sense, but the casual observer leaves something out of his contemplations. The blade of grass has a partner, while the concrete block does not. Let's call the partner simply the *life force*. In concert with the life force, even a blade of grass overcomes fantastic obstacles by *growth*. This growth naturally follows the line of least resistance—it will grow over, under, around, or even through its obstacle!

Reflect on this great truth for a moment: if a blade of grass can unconsciously use the life force to overcome an obviously insurmountable obstacle, how much more can you do with conscious use of an even greater force? The thing we have called *Psycho-Cosmic Power* includes the life force and *all* the power of the universe. It's only necessary to accept and *use* your PCP to sweep away any and all limitations to your progress. This should lead us immediately to a new and wonderfully healthy attitude toward our obstacles and apparent limitations. We now see them merely as *opportunities to demonstrate our mastery of PCP.*

**How to build your launch pad to freedom
from limitation**

In the traditional initiations of the ancient occult orders there was almost invariably one special test that each aspirant was required to undergo:

In the darkness the aspirant is bound hand and foot with sturdy chains, and cast into a dreary chamber full of creeping creatures. He is then left to his own devices, to suffer and die, or to free himself. (Or so the situation appears to the aspirant.) There is a deep lesson for the student who accepts his fate and does nothing. He awakens in the light of morning in extreme physical discomfort, only to discover that the chains are merely flimsy bits of straw which he can break with a mild flexing of his muscles. And the creeping things were only figments of his imagination, the result of simple suggestion. How many of your limitations honestly fit into that category?

The plain fact is *you are limited only by your ability to knowingly declare your PCP to be in operation.* Anything you dare to conceive with PCP you can accomplish!

How PCP disposed of an impossible marital situation

This marriage seemed completely impossible. It was so bad the husband hated to come home. He worked long hours and enrolled in night courses at the local college—anything to avoid the unpleasant atmosphere of the home. He had encountered the basic principles of PCP, and now in desperation he decided to try them. He made the attunement as you have learned in this book, and claimed his birthright of freedom from misery. Then he wound up with a powerful affirmation that kept repeating itself as he went about his daily routine: **Infinite Spirit, like a divine broom, sweeps all unpleasantness out of my life now.** The following Friday evening, he came home from class to find a note from his wife which said, "I've gone to Reno for a divorce." Interestingly enough, the whole thing was financed by another man who subsequently married the woman, leaving not even the normal unpleasant worry about whether the ex-wife would come back some day.

Note here the importance of avoiding negative thoughts and

desires toward the unpleasant condition. You want *freedom*, not punishment for the offensive situation! It turned out to be the best possible release for the wife to run off with another man, but he wasn't entitled to pray for that either. You are always entitled to release, but the method is completely within the prerogative of the Psycho-Cosmic Power!

Dare to desire freedom and it is yours! If you are in a miserable situation, chances are that the other players in your "uncomfortable game" are unhappy, too. So by working to free yourself, you will help them also. There is always a solution that involves the highest good to all parties concerned. The Infinite Cosmic Intelligence behind your PCP has the necessary knowledge and wisdom. You will find the best response from PCP when your motives have been cleansed so you are sure you honestly desire the highest good for all.

Using PCP to break stalemated conditions

Have you ever paused to take a bird's eye view of your life, and decided you're "in a rut"? The growth process is seldom steady. We tend to set a short-term goal, strive for its attainment, then slip back into the doldrums of complacency. Sometimes outward conditions and circumstances seem to gang up on us making us spend vast amounts of energy to get nowhere.

Have you been passed over for promotion recently? Have you made a new friend, or do you see the same old people day after day? How long has it been since you bubbled over with enthusiastic love for your spouse? Have you seriously considered a really new or different idea this week? Do you go from home to work to the same bar and back home every night?

It's easy to get worked up and do something about a situation that really pushes on us. We thrash around energetically, trying to sweep away irritating conditions, but to what end? Is it really an accomplishment to turn off a buzzing alarm clock, only to loll back into a time-wasting sleep? Of course it's good to sweep the negativity out of life, but we can keep it out only by replacing it with vigorous new growth.

If the net effect of your present living seems about equal to taking a healthy whack at a big pillow, it's time to break the stalemate! PCP is a positive help here as always. Whether or not you think you're in a stalemated condition, it's good to use the following exercise for the quietest week of every month:

Sit quietly and make a powerful PCP attunement. Then direct the infinite energy to assist you. Make the following affirmation:

I direct the PCP energy to bring new adventure and unfoldment into my life. It opens new vistas of growth and accomplishment to me now. And I give thanks.

Use the affirmation 50 to 100 times a day for the week, and never forget an expression of thanks for the unexpected Cosmic good that is coming to you!

Then be alert to the opening of wonderful new doors to expression, fulfillment and accomplishment. They are certain to come to you.

How PCP can bring you a new job

Are you completely satisfied with your present position in the business world? If your answer is "yes," I suggest you reread our last section and put it into practice at once—because you're obviously in a rut! But if your answer is "no," it's time to indulge in a bit of self-analysis. Let's begin at the obvious place. What is the nature of your dissatisfaction?

Again, honesty with yourself is of utmost importance. The

degree of your objective understanding of the problem will determine the quality of your solution. There could be many reasons why you are dissatisfied, but let's group them into a few broad categories:

1. Unpleasant social relations or structure.
2. Bored with the humdrum of the routine (you feel a lack of challenge).
3. Desire for more prestige or responsibility.
4. Feel you need more money.

Your "divine discontent" may fall into more than one of these categories. We will treat them individually, but you can work on two or three at the same time. Let's begin by agreeing that a new job certainly isn't the only solution. A change of jobs might only move you from one set of problems to a new and more difficult set. Some people seem to keep doing just that, until they get in so far over their heads that only a miracle can save them. But even if you're in too deep already, judicious use of PCP can bring about your miracle. We will take a good look at each broad category:

1. *Unpleasant social relations or structure.*

We've covered your best solution to this problem already. In Chapter 12, the section on handling special personalities can be applied to any individual or group that seems to be a source of irritation. *Nobody is completely impossible.* However it does take extra effort to get along with the more difficult ones. There are situations where the best course may be to remove yourself, but as often as not you will find that you take your troubles right along. First search your personality carefully. Ask the question, "What is there in *me* that brings out the negativity in my problem relationships?" Ask this in the calm silence of your quiet place and be receptive to the answer that must come from your own subconscious.

Then set out to change *you*. Project yourself into the game with real enthusiasm, and see how much the situation improves. This is another of the times when an all-out effort for 60 days will help you clearly understand the extent of the problem and evaluate the effort necessary to make a go of it. If you still feel a new job is the best solution after 60 days of honest effort, then start looking.

2. *Bored with the routine.*

No position from the lowliest sweeper to the President of General Motors is free from routine and detail. We all chafe under the pressure of the mundane at one time or another. But the real question is, "How well am I discharging the duties and responsibilities of my position?"

"Better than average" is not a good enough answer! Anything less than "excellent" is a definite indication that the problem is in *you* rather than the situation. Again a 60 day test will shed much light. Pitch in and work! Get every detail of your job in the best possible order, then go looking for more. Promise yourself to adopt the attitude of a child, looking with awe at every new situation and idea. See the glamour in the little parts of your job. There can be real satisfaction in turning out a good machined part, a successful trial balance, or even a sparkling clean toilet. Earn the depth of satisfaction that comes from a job well done. Then see if you still need a new job!

3. *Desire for more prestige and/or responsibility.*

The normal desire for growth is very much a part of a healthy, well-balanced existence. It logically includes the desire for growth in responsibility with its corresponding increase in authority and prestige. But do you understand that your present job is the best possible starting point? Application of your best talents and natural ability on *your present job* is a prerequisite to using PCP to get ahead. Using PCP is rather like suing in a court of law. The general rule is, "You must come into a law court with clean hands." In other words, the law will bend over backwards to help a person who has acted in good faith and done everything possible to help himself; but it will offer no help to someone whose negligence or misconduct has contributed to his difficulties. Put forth the *effort to help yourself*, then you are ready to apply PCP to bring even greater progress.

4. *Feel you need more money.*

This, too, is a normal and healthy desire. In our economically oriented society we are expected to *earn* our own way, but there are many different ways that money can be earned. Obviously a $210,000-a-year corporation president doesn't turn out 30 times the volume of work as a $7,000 a year machinist, but each earns his wage by application of the talents he has developed. It is reasonable and proper to use PCP to increase your effectiveness on your present job, and to develop the latent talents that will lead to better and better positions. Although the corporation president doesn't turn out 30 times the work of his machinist, he may be personally responsible for bringing the firm better than 300 times the profit. Each man moves in the circles best suited to his abilities, and the effectiveness of each contributes to the success of the business as a whole. Play the game according to its rules! Work diligently for the good of your company, speak well of it, and pray for its continued growth and prosperity. Thus you will get the best results from applying Psycho-Cosmic Power to increase your income.

Make your attunement and speak to the PCP energy within you:

I direct the Psycho-Cosmic Power to express through me as ever increasing effectiveness on my job, and in my income producing ability. It is working to increase my present wages while grooming me for promotion after promotion. I give thanks for my ever increasing income.

What of the "unfortunate" person who finds himself temporarily out of work? I chose the term "unfortunate" on purpose because that is the way we generally feel. But that's the first mistake! To apply the adjective "unfortunate" to yourself is to deny the effectiveness of the PCP energies, and thus cut yourself off from the source of all help. The only intelligent attitude to adopt is: *I give my heartfelt thanks for this wonderful opportunity to advance to a better position.*

Let a feeling of happy expectancy fill your being. You can't go out looking for work while projecting a negative expectancy. That will keep you occupied with lesser jobs, but repel the good one that is seeking you. Instead, work on your attitude while applying your PCP in a completely positive manner. Feel the joy of PCP attunement and affirm:

The infinite PCP energy surges through my being, making me into a perfect magnet which irresistibly attracts my ideal position. This wonderful new job will be an excellent outlet for my talents and will challenge me to develop new ones. I know this perfect job is seeking me even as I seek it, and I will contribute handsomely to the growth and effectiveness of my new company. I give thanks for my new job now.

Then follow the guidance to your perfect position. It will work for you!

How PCP can release you from a bad marriage

In Chapter 13 we talked about how to attract and hold your perfect mate. But what if you find yourself trapped in an impossible marriage? There are lessons you must learn from the situation before it's either safe or proper to use PCP to free yourself. Let's make a simple checklist to be sure:

1. How did you get into this mess?
2. Have you tried everything possible to make it work?
3. Are you willing to pay the price of freedom, both in money and loneliness?

Again it's important to do your analysis with care—that's the only way to avoid winding up in a worse mess than the one you're trying to get out of. We'll look at them one by one.

1. *How did you get into this mess?*

It happens to many couples, a week or thirty years after the wedding. You wake up some morning and each realize that the person across the table is a complete stranger—you have about as much business being married to each other as to Magilla Gorilla! How did this happen to you? And how can you be sure it won't happen again, if you get out of this one?

A review of our last chapter's section on the courtship period will help you understand the nature of the complete compatibility that is essential to a happy marriage. Do you understand how you reacted blindly to infatuation, and failed to look for the lasting ties of common attitudes, common religious and economic appetites, and the blending of vibration that makes the mere sharing of presence a joy? You may be right that there is no hope for this present marriage, but do you understand the necessity of planning to grow together instead of apart? Meditate carefully, and be certain of your ability to avoid the same mistakes again. This is important even if you think you will never remarry! Companionship is essential to a normal life, and if you are normal you will very probably marry again.

2. *Have you tried everything possible to make it work?*

We often hear of couples who divorce, then later remarry and find a very pleasant life together. What are the good qualities in your spouse that attracted you to each other in the first place? Perhaps you've been grating on each other for so long there are open wounds which just need a little time to heal. It's sometimes good to try a trial separation. This is another kind of 60 day test that is best attempted as a last resort before beginning actual divorce proceedings. If you both act like adults, meet only when necessary during the period and then go out of the way to be nice to each other, you may find a completely changed atmosphere when you finally try a reunion. Be sure you don't make the mistake of breaking up what might turn into an ideal marriage.

3. *Are you willing to pay the price of freedom, both in money and loneliness?*

It's important to realize that, even with the tremendous power of PCP working for you, there is still a price for divorce. There is a period of severe emotional stress, no matter how relieved you think you'll feel. And there is immediate financial strain as well. When one family becomes two, with two rents, two telephones, two utilities, two entertainment requirements, and on and on; there will naturally be less money for each of you. Or how about the property settlement? Do you realize that what seems perfectly fair to you may be completely unreasonable from the standpoint of your about to be ex-spouse? *Be sure you're willing to pay the price before you use PCP.*

The time for turning to PCP

When you're convinced that you are making the right move, that you can avoid repeating the mistake, and you're willing to pay the price; it's time to turn to the Psycho-Cosmic Power for your solution. Make your attunement in the peace and quiet of your meditation chamber, and talk to the PCP energy. Say,

Infinite Spirit, it seems I have made a serious mistake and tied myself up in a miserable marriage. But, Great Life Force, that's the reason men put erasers on their pencils. I know my spouse is just as uncomfortable as I am, and I seek relief for both of us. I direct the infinite PCP energy to bring about an immediate release in the form of a solution that brings the highest good for everyone concerned.

Make your attunement every morning and evening, and repeat your directions to the PCP energy until you succeed.

Strive to follow the guidance, and cooperate with the help that is certain to come to you. Take no rash actions, and be willing to spend time in the negotiating and bargaining that may be required to properly wind up your arrangements. But be sure the parting holds no bitterness for you—you can't afford that emotion. Enjoy your new freedom! And rejoice in your ex's new happiness also.

Points to Remember from This Chapter

1. You can overcome any obstacle by growth in your personal PCP.

2. You are limited only by your ability to conceive Cosmic solutions to life's problems.

3. Stress *freedom*, not desire to punish the limiting factors.

4. Apply PCP to one week out of every month to stir up new situations and stimulants to growth.

5. Let PCP bring you the right job, a perfect marriage, or whatever you need to progress.

chapter **15**

how to

Turn Surrender or Defeat into Smashing Victory

We've all used the expression, "He could fall into the gutter and come out wearing a new suit of clothes!" We meant to imply that the person has some kind of special "luck" or ability to snatch victory from the very brink of failure. Do people think that about you? Don't you wish you could believe it about yourself? Let's lay the groundwork for a powerful *victory complex* through PCP.

Victory or defeat is dependent on a state of mind

During the two decades immediately following World War II, many political cartoons were inspired by this country's foreign aid program. One of the favorite themes was a caricature of a Latin American dictator addressing his cabinet with the caption, "The only way out of our financial crisis is to declare war on the United States and immediately surrender." Ignoring the political implications, the difference in point of view as to who actually wins a war is worthy of considerable contemplation.

The Master had a choice comment on this subject: "For what is a man profited, if he shall gain the whole world, and lose his own soul?" (Matt. 16:26.)

In the Taoist traditions of the ancient Chinese oracle, the *I Ching,* our existence is explained as the cyclical ebb and flow of the light and dark principles, *Yang* and *Yin.* We are urged to amplify our opportunities in life by making use of the tide—by striving with real diligence when the light forces are advancing, and conserving our energies during the dark periods when success is denied us by the times. There are many instructions in timing in the *I Ching,* but the deeper lesson is the understanding that *seeming defeat is the greatest stepping stone to victory,* even as victory unguarded is the prelude to defeat. It's not some seeming catastrophe that affects you, but the continuing quality of your attitude and thought that controls the unfolding of your destiny.

Men even go so far as to blame their troubles on God. For a typical but horrible example, I quote a bit of language used to describe Proposition 5 on the November, 8, 1966 California General Election Ballot: ". . . when property is damaged or destroyed after the lien date (the first Monday in March of any year) by fire, flood, earthquake, *or other act of God,* the Legislature is permitted to provide for any appropriate relief . . ." The very laws of our land blame major disasters on God! We speak of *brainwashing* as a terrible practice limited to use by despotic, tyrannical dictatorships. But man's folly of blaming a completely benevolent Deity for his mistakes of getting in nature's way is brainwashing of the worst sort. Were the name of a "living" man used instead of the term God, there would be slander suits filed in courts all over the land. But we stupidly stand by and assent to the slander of the Living God!

If you're not completely affronted by the legal term, *act of God,* you are still living a life of fear and ineffectiveness. Disaster and humiliating defeat lurk all around as long as you remain under the spell of that brainwashing. Tell yourself over and over until it becomes a part of your being:

God, Cosmic Good, is all love and all good; man's misfortunes are the result of his improper use of natural law—they are never malevolent acts of a despotic deity.

The cause of misfortune

All troubles can be easily understood in the simple terms of the *I Ching*. When man tries to move counter to the flow of the great tides of life, he must do so with the utmost preparation and care or he will meet with "misfortune." When a hurricane strikes the coast of Florida, there is widespread destruction which man calls a disaster. But the structures that were built to withstand periodic onslaughts of hurricane weather, and the people who stayed prudently in them, come through un-scathed. Why don't you call the people who were less than prudent *foolish*, and rejoice in the *benevolent act of God* which "saved" the ones who stayed in the safely built buildings? No! Man egotistically claims credit for the "good" things that happen to him—these are his "accomplishments." But he child-ishly blames God for his mistakes. It's like the days when my boys were four and five years old. You would hear a loud crash of a glass or dish in the other room. When you rushed in to see what had happened, there were two boys each pointing a finger at the other and shouting, "He did it!"

We grown-ups think this is a completely infantile action in our children. Then we turn around and even write it into our statute books— "It wasn't my stupidity or foolishness. God did it!" Look at nature in its infinite wisdom and abundance, and see how ridiculous man must seem in comparison. Almost every year there are huge brush fires in Southern California which naturally burn one or more of the houses that were built in the danger area. Again man cries, "Disaster!" But what of nature? Nature knows that the climate of the area runs to long, hot, rainless summers which inevitably lead to fire in the dry brush area. So there are species of plants growing here which produce seeds that germinate only after being exposed to the tremendous heat of a brush fire. Thus the plants live in peaceful, uncrowded conditions until destroyed by rampaging fire, but the very destruction triggers the reseeding process for the new beginning.

No "disaster" is bad for everybody. From every misfortune comes some sort of a new beginning. We know of the germination of seeds caused by the brush fire, but even the great earthquake that rocked Southern California in the early thirties brought good, Cosmic Good. It was the real beginning of the prosperity of the giant construction industry which not only repaired and rebuilt what had been destroyed, but went on to build and build and build and produce an area of "civilization" totally undreamed of by the pre-earthquake population. Thus works PCP, when understood.

The value of defeat

No defeat is all bad! Our Vedanta brothers, whom we call Hindus, can shed much light on this. One of their principal deities is the goddess Shiva (or Siva), who is called the *destroyer*. You may ask how anyone in his right mind can worship a goddess of destruction. But the Hindu understands this as the *destruction which clears the way for new growth,* and the Western mind might better understand Shiva as the goddess of progress. Since the Vedanta devotees also accept the concept of reincarnation, they look on the change we call "death" as the mere shedding of the old body to prepare for rest and a new birth. This is beautifully put in their immortal scripture, the Bhagavad-Gita, when Krishna says,

. . . as when one lays his worn out clothes away, and taking new ones says, "I will wear these today." So the spirit lightly puts down its garb of flesh, and lightly passes on to inherit a body fresh. . . . This is Cosmic Wisdom.

There is hidden value in every disaster, and in every personal defeat. Lessons of "togetherness" and teamwork benefit the species whenever emergencies force men to strive together to rescue and care for survivors or otherwise minimize the effects of catastrophe. Even war brings men great stimulation to selfless acts, and forces them to work together in a common cause recognized as more important than any single individual. We may feel this is small recompense for the carnage of war or natural disaster. But by contemplating the concept of reincarnation, we may get a faint glimmering of the undying reality that is both the "soul" of man and the Creator of the Universe. Cosmic wisdom works in many mysterious ways for our true benefit!

Psychic or spiritual help is the underlying cause of many personal defeats and failures!

This sounds like an utterly ridiculous assertion, but let's take a deeper look at its meaning.

For well over a year, an officer of a small corporation was involved in an intimate relationship with a very personable woman. They were seriously planning marriage, but the divorce laws of the state kept him from legally consummating the wedding. He complained bitterly about the harsh laws that kept people from living naturally, and constantly heckled his attorney to find some way to speed up the legal process. Finally it was just four months before he could have his final decree, and he looked forward eagerly to a more normal existence. Meanwhile his company was purchased by a major corporation, which set out to eliminate duplication of management people.

He was given very generous notice of termination and immediately began seeking a new position. With the help of his fiancée, he sent out hundreds of résumés and got interviews for many very good positions. But something seemed to keep him from landing any of them! Finally the day came when he was actually out of a job, and he jokingly painted a picture of abject poverty to his fiancée. Immediately the girl disappeared out of his life—she dropped him like he had leprosy or worse!

Now the executive was at rock bottom. He sat quietly contemplating his predicament, and asking how he had misused the universal powers to wind up in this fix. As he sat in quiet thought, he seemed to hear a voice inside his head. It was laughing as it said, "We had to find some way to show you that you would only come to grief by marrying that woman. Now go out and look for a job, and prepare yourself to meet your true helpmate." He followed instructions, landed an excellent position, and now enjoys the companionship of a truly devoted and loving wife. Out of the depths of defeat came greater victory!

How to look for the lesson in a setback

We cling tenaciously to our limitations in the misguided belief that they are blessings. Then when our higher self forces the issue and sweeps away the spiritually unnecessary conditions, we are tempted to wail and bemoan our fate. We want to sit and sob, "Why did this have to happen to me?" But we must not give in to this terrible urge! Instead look for the lesson of the setback through your PCP!

What if the setback is the death of a loved one? This is probably the hardest tragedy to take, but a little detached meditation will help here, too. Can your grief possibly help the departed soul? Put yourself in the position of your departed loved one. You are deprived of the physical horse you rode through earth life, and face the adjustment to a new situation. Your love for your friends and relatives left on earth is of course unabated. You look back and see them wallowing in grief and misery, and you long to comfort them; but without a physical instrument you feel completely powerless to reach them. Thus you suffer much more in their reflected grief than you do for your own loss of a physical horse. Is it fair to your departing loved one to add the frustration of inability to comfort you to his many new problems? There is only one answer! *You must release the departed in love, and pray for his (or her) progress on the higher Cosmic planes of life.*

And so it is with all our lesser tragedies! The only intelligent course is to release in love whatever you may lose, and then continue the business of living. It's only by clinging to dead issues and things of the past that we experience defeat. Instead, look to today and tomorrow. What is your best course to resurrect growth, and snatch victory out of decay and defeat? Isn't it logical to use your PCP?

Demand that PCP bring victory, but don't limit its form

If there is ever a time when we are completely unqualified to assess our position, it's the period immediately following a major personal setback. No matter how great your inner strength, there is an emotional reaction—a letdown! There is no blocking the reaction for 99 people out of 100, but what you do from there is the most important choice of life. In the great occult traditions, we are taught to be so "unattached" to the people and things of our life that there can be no emotional letdown of the type we are discussing. But we live in a different time and way from those who may have been able to live in such a completely unattached manner. So we must learn to do the next best thing, or isn't it perhaps a more alive thing anyway? Let's go ahead and enter into the emotional spirit of life, giving of ourselves to the fullest. Then when we feel the emotional props knocked out from under us by a major setback, do what comes naturally. Fall. But don't just lie there, bounce back with PCP! It's that simple ability to *bounce* that is the secret of turning any defeat into glorious victory!

How shall you go about bouncing back? First, simply accept the fact of the apparent misfortune. Physical facts are real, and no bit of metaphysical gymnastics can change them. You may manage to grow a new arm or leg if you need one, but the growth process takes time. Accept the objective facts and get the emotional reaction out of your system as quickly as possible. At all cost, you must avoid the "Why did this have to happen to me?" routine! Rely on Cosmic Good to be revealed! The technique is to get the disaster out of your mind and replace it with psychic truth! Once you accept the facts, and agree with yourself that there is nothing more to be done on that specific issue, the rest is easy.

Busy yourself with the routine things of daily life. Attack some small project that has needed your attention but you have been putting off 'till later. Light-hearted entertainment can be a big help if you are inclined in that direction. Any good company and light entertainment will help. The point is to seek any and all activities that will help you bounce back toward your happy self.

As soon as you make the start, we can use PCP to finish the job. Enjoy yourself as long as you feel it's necessary. Then when you are alone, it's time to sit quietly and apply your PCP. Use the mystic mantra to make your attunement as usual. When you feel it reaching a peak, talk to the PCP energy:

Infinite Psycho-Cosmic Power, I give thanks for this wonderful opportunity to demonstrate your effectiveness. I know that my apparent loss is merely preparation for greater accomplishments and glorious victory. I accept your perfect help, and thank you for your manifestation of the highest good in my life now!"

Then go about your daily routine in happy expectation. A friend and student had recently suffered through a long and harrowing series of family financial reverses. Then she decided it was time to use PCP to do something about it. She wrote this with bubbling enthusiasm:

> The beauty shop is almost ready to open. I'll send you an "invite," and I do hope, above everyone else, that you will come to see just what in my case "faith" has done. Each day of this project I have tuned in on the PCP lights, and especially in the area of prosperity. Money has been coming in to me to finance this shop from unbelievable sources—it hasn't stopped! Everything I have needed *and more* is done, including one extravagance. I could not have done this alone, and I'm not talking about physical labor! I have kept my sights constantly on the end result with absolute surety that it would happen exactly that way, and it has. Every single person, no matter how insignificant the area of contact, has seemed to bend over backwards to help me. Salespersons, business people, everyone has been just great. I have never felt so positive about anything, and had so much fun doing it. Thanks to my Guidance! No one will ever convince me that faith is not the essence—I'll show them my beauty shop! I have the profound feeling that I'm on the right track and that one area of my personal Karma is accounted for. It would take pages to relate all my wonderful experiences concerning this shop, and I've dedicated it to all my Spirit Teachers in thanks and as visible evidence of their help.

The victorious Cosmic life is yours now

Happy expectation serves as a perfect vehicle for the working of PCP energy in your life. Maintain careful watch on your feelings and attitude—you must expect the best always. But this doesn't mean you can lie back on your couch while you are expecting! The key to all victory and success is one tiny word, WORK! Your expectant attitude gives you the emotional freedom necessary to maximum effectiveness, but only the APPLICATION of your whole being to each task brings accomplishment. Practice *accomplishment* in every activity you begin. In the eyes of the Infinite, the smallest and the greatest tasks a human can imagine are of equal magnitude. What is the accomplishment of either when compared with the creation of the whole universe? The habit of success you develop by completing your lesser undertakings will carry over into all areas of your life.

Train yourself to consciously apply PCP to each job you start, and keep it "turned on" until you finish. It's just as easy to develop the habit of success as failure. Start now, and let PCP bring your highest good!

Points to Remember from This Chapter

1. No tragedy is an "act of God." It is a result of man's foolishness, and ignorance of PCP.

2. We must look upon defeat as merely the destruction of error that clears the way for new growth.

3. We must stop clinging to our limitations in the misguided belief they are blessings.

4. Learn to bounce back from defeat to glorious victory with PCP.

5. Build a success complex by using PCP to complete every task you start.

chapter **16**

how to

Use PCP to Perfect Your Personal Relationship to Cosmic Good

No less a personality than the master psychiatrist Carl G. Jung commented that every patient he really helped came away with a closer relationship to God, Cosmic Good. We have worked for fifteen chapters on the *impersonal* laws governing Psycho-Cosmic Power; now let's turn our attention to the purely *personal* side for deeper understanding of PCP for Cosmic Good.

Who are you?

Our psychologist and psychiatrist friends delight in posing the simple question, "Who are you?" This is of course a "trick" question, designed to determine your mental-emotional polarization. One's instinctive answer would probably be his (or her) own name, but the psychologist would consider this shallow and self-centered. Or if a woman answered, "Mrs. (her husband's first and last name)," she would be considered overly dominated by her spouse. The trick to the question is that the questioner is really asking, "*What* are you?"

Before venturing an answer to this translated version of the question, let's look at a Cosmic comment from the Bible: *What is man that thou art mindful of him? And the son of man, that thou visitest him? For thou hast made him a little lower than the angels, and hast crowned him with glory and honor. Thou madest him to have dominion over the works of thy hands; thou hast put all things under his feet.* (Psalm 8:3–6.)

You've had enough exposure to PCP by now to understand that there is more to our universe than scientific man yet imagines, and there is one underlying creative force behind the whole of it. We can best answer the "Who are you" question with a look at the Cosmic beginnings of the Judeo-Christian tradition: *And God said, Let us make man in our image and after our likeness: and let him have dominion over the fish of the sea, and over the fowl of the air, and over the cattle, and over all the earth, and over every creeping thing that creepeth upon the earth. So God created man in his own image, in the image of God created he him; male and female created he them. And God blessed them, and God said unto them, Be fruitful, and multiply, and replenish the earth, and subdue it. . . .* (Genesis 1:26–28.)

The use of the word *replenish* is worthy of careful meditation. Does this mean there were men on earth before the Creation Story? If so what happened to them? Some digging in the Genesis story will reveal many other Cosmic clues indicating that there were "other men" already dwelling on our little planet at the time of the "Creation." Perhaps all this is to show us that only a purely metaphysical interpretation is implied, with no historical significance at all. It will have the same personal meaning to us as Jesus' classic metaphysical statement: "Verily, verily, I say unto you, Before Abraham was, I am." (John 8:58.)

Aren't we told that Jesus came to earth to be our great example? But consider carefully, great example of what? In the words of today, the example was the compassion, power and fullness that comes from a totally personal relationship to God. The message was regularly given: *Seek ye first the Kingdom of God . . . and all things shall be added unto you.* But where is this Kingdom of God? A reasonable person must conclude *it is in your own heart!*

With this bit of background, let's hazard our own Cosmic answer to the *who are you* thing. How about: I am an amateur, studying in this earthly classroom to learn to be a professional.

What does it take to become a professional? First let's reexamine the idea of being created in the "image and likeness" of God. We concluded that this part of the Bible is clearly metaphysical, rather than expository. Obviously God is not a great big human shaped monster who has made a bunch of little puppets to run around looking like himself. We must be talking about something else—and it's that something else that makes you a god.

Let's look in on another conversation: *The Jews answered him, saying, For a good work we stone thee not; but for blasphemy; and because that thou, being a man, makest thyself God. Jesus answered them, Is it not written in your law, I said, ye are gods? If he called them gods, unto whom the word of God came, and the scripture cannot be broken; Say ye of him, whom the Father hath sanctified, and sent into the world, Thou blasphemest; because I said, I am the Son of God?* (John 10:33–36.)

If you are in the "image and likeness" of God, aren't you also a "Son of God?" But what is that image? Let's dodge the confusion created by the Hebrews' refusal to admit the female portion of the Godhead, and their substitution of an indefinable something called the "Holy Ghost." In all major religions there is a Trinity concept of God. This is easily understood as the creative triangle; Father, Mother, Child. To the occult world the similar triangle would be light, love, and power. In you the Cosmic trinity becomes Intellect, Receptivity, and Manifestation; or Mind, Soul, Body. At different times in our daily activities it becomes necessary to polarize or center our consciousness on different points of our personal triangle. Let's look at the game of life from this new vantage point.

How to play the great game of life

Every activity in life is some sort of a game. There are psychological games, mental games, physical games, and a great variety of games we call economic pursuits. The broad view of life explains why. This earthly sojourn is a day, or perhaps a semester, in the great universal school. Its purpose is the evolution of YOU as a whole being. At our present level of evolution, we are like young children in the great scheme of things. How are children taught the simple lessons of social conduct and expansion of their world of experience? Simple games are best because they keep attention and interest sustained better than any other teaching activity.

And so it is with us little children of the Cosmic universe. We come to this earth to grow by expansion of our Cosmic experience. Just as in the earth schools we organize for our offspring, this Cosmic universal school is graded in its difficulty. It requires the demonstration of certain minimum degrees of proficiency before one may be "promoted" to the next class or to the university. So we progress from social child's games, through the game of earth schools, then college, then the fascinating game of business with its own multigraded sets of subgames. And as a corollary, we play at romance, war, marriage, parenthood, divorce, remarriage, country club or tract living, and many more.

This brings us to a trite old quote which is still worthy of consideration here: "It isn't whether you win or lose, but how you play the game." The rewards of winning seem to outweigh anything else! After all, they include wealth, prestige, fame, popularity, and even adoration. What child would trade some portion of these things for depth of character, spiritual growth, or the vague promise of a better life in some future incarnation? But in the larger sense, there are no losers in life's important games. It's just that some people seem to reap greater benefits than others of the same ability and application.

An interesting example of this is the pre-merger days of the National and American football leagues. In the competition for talent a year or two before the merger, a topflight graduating senior quarterback could hope for a three year contract for an aggregate consideration approaching a million dollars. But the following year, when the merger had limited the bargaining power of the young athletes, quarterbacks of similar ability were going for a fourth of that figure. Differences of a strictly timing or "lucky break" nature are probably the result of "carry-overs" of things earned in previous lifetimes of our Cosmic existences. Still the best policy is to accept the good graciously, and bend with the negative with Cosmic grace. It's very like the peculiar bounce which may decide a close football game. The bounce may give you victory, but it's just as certainly true that hard work and application kept you in position to take advantage of the opportunity. To recover an opponent's fumble when your team is trailing 64 to 0 would be a very small consolation. Thus it's the business of "staying in the game" that should concern us here.

How to use the Cosmic Trinity for help

Let's look back at the Cosmic Trinity idea for help. We used the terms Intellect, Receptivity, and Manifestation. In this context we might substitute Judgment, Enthusiasm, and Effective Action for the three points of the triangle. We are simply saying that the key to effective action is enthusiasm moving under control of good judgment. Without enthusiasm and its resultant energy, all the good judgment in the world will just sit idle. There are positive and negative forms of enthusiasm just as there are of judgment, but we seldom think in those terms. You often hear it said that someone exercised "bad" judgment, but have you ever heard of someone exhibiting "bad" enthusiasm? The reason is we have a different word for it. Positive enthusiasm is the eagerness to give of the self, to put all of yourself into something for the sheer joy of the doing. Its opposite is the unwillingness to give of the self, based on fear of the outcome, that we call *anxiety*.

Enthusiasm is loose and flexible, willing to *do* in the most intense manner, but never tied up in knots. While anxiety is tense and inflexible, either trying too hard or not trying at all—both forms of action being based on fear of failure. In the games of life, whether football, business, war, or romance, there is plenty of room for enthusiasm and no room for its opposite. We can see that enthusiasm is related to love in its givingness, while anxiety is related to hatred which is itself only another form of fear. Everyone knows it's much easier to generate enthusiasm in a child than in an adult. The Master told us the same thing: *Except ye become as a little child, ye cannot enter the Kingdom of Heaven.* It's really a simple statement of the relative merits of enthusiasm and anxiety. Except ye play the game of life with the enthusiasm of a child, you will suffer the defeats of tension and anxiety. In the vernacular of today, you will beat yourself!

The tremendous force we discussed throughout this book is nothing more than universal Cosmic enthusiasm. When you become enthusiastic you automatically tune your being to the Psycho-Cosmic Power, and attract whatever energy you may need for accomplishment. This power of attracting PCP through your enthusiasm is all the natural ability you need to play any of the wonderful games of life. Now we have the energy and ability, we need only the soundness of judgment to insure our continually effective action. Again it will serve our purpose to borrow from the lessons of recognized games. If you want to learn a new game, the essential element is a *coach*. Depending on the importance the community places on the particular game, you may find one or more professional coaches, or the teaching may be left to an older player or even a contemporary with a smattering of knowledge of the rules and execution. Or in some extreme cases you may find that you must serve as your own coach. In any event, the coach initially supplies the missing judgment factor—the controlling influence that turns enthusiasm from undisciplined chaos into invincible effectiveness.

We might define victory in any game as the *result of natural ability made effective through proper coaching*. Now here's the meat of this discussion. The question to ask yourself is: *Where am I getting my coaching?* Would you be more effective working under a Cosmic coach? In general, man believes that effective coaching greatly improves the value of a player. In this way we see the growth of the great football powers on the university scene. Once a head coach has attained the reputation as a great developer of players, the problem of recruiting new talent from the high schools is greatly simplified, and players who might be first string at many other schools will sit on the bench and wait their turn as long as they are on the great man's team.

How would you like a chance to play for the greatest Coach in the universe? Whether you realize it or not, you are on His team already. You were born on His team! And if you make "first string," you're guaranteed a winning season! There's no better attitude to take toward God, Cosmic Good, than that of a player to his head coach.

How to earn God's special attention

It will help our understanding to carry the coaching analogy a little farther. When the player arrives on campus as a freshman he has a long way to go before he plays directly for the varsity head coach. His first year is spent on the freshman team, where the instruction is carried out entirely by assistant coaches. But these assistants are part of the head coach's organization, and are picked for their own ability to bring out the latent talent in each of their charges. A good player must pay attention to the assistant coaches, and he will learn much from them.

Your own High Self and your Cosmic spirit teachers are the assistant coaches on this team, and their success depends on how well they are able to help you develop your natural talents and ability. When the time comes, the Head Coach will rely heavily on their judgment as to your readiness to try out for the "first team." How can you best insure your chance to work directly for the Head Coach? Can it be anything except do *your best to learn,* and *play well right where you are?*

Learn well your Cosmic fundamentals as set out in this book. Good execution on the playing field of life will win your coach's positive attention. The more effectively you strive, the more interest you naturally attract from the coaching staff. *Nothing is more important than earning the confidence and respect of this "Head Coach."* Like the personal interest from a head coach to each of his first team players, there is a special personal interest from God to those few souls whose striving has earned them a berth on the spiritual first string. The reward is a new dimension of livingness brought about by a continuing mystic experience.

How to prepare for mystic experience

Regardless of the effort and apparent sacrifice that might be required, the deep mystical experience is well worth any price. I prefer to call it the realization of your personal relationship with God and the *experience of its reciprocal nature.* As is so often the case in spiritual striving, the price itself is a pleasure to pay. It's the striving for Cosmic attunement with all of Creation that has been the subject of all our previous work in this book with the Psycho-Cosmic Power. In the old occult traditions the first step is to "purify the temple," which is to say, purify and cleanse your body, mind, and spirit. But isn't this the broad concept of the work of the first fifteen chapters in this book? And can't we logically conclude that anything which contributes to the improvement of your health, happiness, material well-being, or spiritual growth is a means of purifying that temple? As you do your best to improve all areas of life, you are readying yourself for the great experience.

The next positive step is to set a regular time and place for your daily meditation period. Even if your way of making a living requires much travel or a completely irregular schedule, there is still no excuse to miss. The best time for most of us is just after arising in the morning. The natural reaction to this is, "But I don't have time!" Nonsense! Just get up fifteen minutes earlier! That fifteen minutes spent in meditation and communing with the creative Cosmic energy of the universe is worth much more to your well-being than a little lost sleep. It's like building a new brick house by adding one brick each day. You may not see startling results at first, but the goal is worth waiting for, and the final result can be achieved by perseverance.

Open each morning's meditation by calling on your High Self and your Spirit Teachers to help improve your attunement with them and with the PCP energies. Tell them you seek their help in attaining your personal relationship with God. Then repeat a simple prayer from the heart. It will take different forms for different people, but mine would go something like this:

Heavenly Father, the spark of your own essence in me cries out for your companionship. Please grant me some small touch of the personal element of yourself. I sit in the silence savoring the joy of this answered prayer.

What form will your answer take? The answers are as varied as the possible shadings of the colors of the rainbow. Attempts to express the feeling that comes with this experience range from a middle-aged woman's comment, "Suddenly I knew deep down inside that I was one with God," to Walt Whitman's *Leaves of Grass* with its earthy descriptions of that perfect oneness with all of creation that we might call the ideal mystic experience. Consider some testimonies:

Some Cosmic attunement experiences

A lady from the South wrote me about one of her experiences:

> While I was sitting in meditation, a beautiful thing happened to me. Exquisite colors filled the room, coming and going in ever changing brilliance. My arms turned a beautiful light purple, and everywhere there was color. Then I was in the presence of a spirit, and now I know who it is. It's me!

For contrast, a gentleman from the Midwest described his experience:

> One day I was out in the yard thinking, if only I could see an opening to heaven. Suddenly a black door came down at me. At first I thought it was a cloud, then I realized a cloud couldn't be square on all four corners. And I saw that what I thought was black was

really an open door, and I knew inside I had received my perfect answer straight from God.

Still another said:

This morning I found out something wonderful. I don't have to look in the mirror to see or feel the love light of our Father-Mother-Son. I can see it all around me and feel the love so in my heart. You see, I've been saying: Help me, Father, or Thank you for letting me see the light. I found out asking for myself I couldn't quite feel the love of God, yet I did to a certain amount. But when I ask God to send his light to all of us—to all his people—I feel him down to my toes.

The most common factor in all the experiences confided to me seems to be some experience of *light. The mystical light is real!* Seek it with all your heart! Once you have found it, you will be changed forever.

Your life *after* the Cosmic mystic experience

Naturally there are many levels or degrees of the mystic experience, and you may go through one, several, or even hundreds in this lifetime. Each experience of the Cosmic Oneness will have a definite changing effect on your character and outlook. Certainly each contact will leave you with a greater feeling of your personal brotherhood with all creatures of the earth. But there are pitfalls even here! An attunement contact may be so overwhelmingly beautiful that you may be temporarily dazed. We are all vividly surprised at the moment of the first experience, but we must strive to recover quickly.

One small example may convey much more than thousands of words of explanation. We were friendly with an elderly woman who lived by herself in a bachelor apartment. After a deep mystic experience, she felt her brotherhood with all creatures so keenly that she couldn't permit herself to kill anything. A family of mice occupied one corner of her room, and she fed her "little friends" daily. Perhaps this would have been all right by itself, but the same courtesy was also shown to cockroaches, ants, flies, and silverfish. With such good treatment, these household pests multiplied and flourished until the landlord put his foot down.

And we are told that the most celebrated of American mystics, Walt Whitman, remained so out of balance from his tastes of the Cosmic experience that his personal life was a shambles. *We must strive to maintain our effectiveness in this life as our best gift to our fellow men.* How can we expect to explain the great value of the mystic experience and thus share it with our fellow creatures, if the example of our own life is some kind of starry-eyed self-delusion? You owe it to the mortal world to avoid going to extremes because you sit dazzled by the wonder of the experience.

In the Hindu classic, the Bhagavad-Gita, God incarnated as Krishna gives Arjuna the mystic experience in great wonder and glory. But He expects Arjuna to *immediately* go back into the great battle of his mundane or worldly life and *fight effectively to win Cosmic Good.* He is guaranteed victory by the power of his Cosmic experience, *but only if he refuses to let it put him out of balance.* And so it is with your life. The whole power of the universe is waiting to manifest through you—if you will keep your balance and *use it!*

In the prayer left to his followers, Jesus included the idea: *And lead us not into temptation . . .* Since all of life is full of little temptations, we can be sure this is not to be taken literally. Metaphysically it brings us the same message we received from Krishna. The prayer is for strength to keep our balance—*Lead me into the great mystic experience, but let me not succumb to the temptation to let it overwhelm me.* Keep your balance so you can intelligently share your sublime experience with the world.

Your responsibility with Cosmic mystic life

Let's pause and examine the responsibility that comes with the mystic life. When you realize your perfect oneness with God and all Cosmic creation, you know that every creature is a part of you. You will feel a personal responsibility for the growth and well being of mankind as a whole and for each individual soul struggling for its own release into the Cosmic light. You will experience the pain of offering this light to many, only to see them reject it. But there will also be the joy of seeing the growth of someone you managed to inspire.

We must plant tiny seeds in the soil of the race subconscious mind, and be content with the certain knowledge that they will sprout and bear fruit in their own time—even if we never know of it in person. It's certainly a truism that the more effectively you share your knowledge, the greater will be your own growth. In the great tradition of the Buddha, the truly selfless mystic pledges to renounce the joys of permanent Nirvana until his efforts have opened the gates to the lowliest soul still struggling on earth. And this very renunciation so endears him to the Creator of the Universe that he touches the fringes of another dimension even higher than the supreme mystic experience. And what is that? Live in the COSMIC LIGHT and work for the enlightenment of mankind—then at the right time in Cosmic truth you will know what.

Points to Remember from This Chapter

1. You are an amateur, studying in this earthly classroom to learn to be a professional in Cosmic science.

2. You are most effective when you play the great game of life with relaxed enthusiasm and faith in PCP.

3. Victory in any game, as in life, is the result of native ability made effective through proper training.

4. Recognize God, Cosmic Good, as your "Head Coach," but pay attention to the assistant coaches as well. They are your own High Self and your Spirit Teachers.

5. Ask God and your Spirit Teachers for your mystic experience at each morning's meditation.

6. After your own wonderful experience, *keep your mental balance* and intelligently use it in your contacts with the "everyday" world.

how to

Use PCP To Open New Doors of Expression, Fulfillment, and Accomplishment

Since we are about to discuss the climaxing of your own Cosmic growth, it seems fitting to share some of my experience with you.

My first book, *The Miraculous Laws of Universal Dynamics,* seems a good place to start. I had no conscious idea of writing a book, but my very modest efforts to help others by sharing the tiny bit of light I had discovered lead to an inquiry from the publisher. Next the very process of organizing and presenting the light, as I was able to see it then, opened new doors of growth and expression. This development continued and made it mandatory that I present another "dimension" in the second book, *Helping Yourself with E.S.P.*

The growth resulting from the effort of writing the second book caused me to reach a startling conclusion. Though I stressed *balance* as the basic theme of each, each was out of balance in its own way. Thus it became necessary to produce

Helping Yourself with Psycho-Cosmic Power to present the higher truth that resolves the paradox. And again, the writing of this book has led to personal development more wonderful than anything I dared dream. This isn't intended to be idle boasting, but a personal testimonial to the tremendous rewards of learning to be a conscious instrument for the expression of the great Psycho-Cosmic Power. This is the theme we need to carry over into your daily life.

Your new power to achieve

We set up programs in this book for the workings of the PCP energies and found them a priceless asset to any undertaking. Then we discussed the seeking of your personal mystic experience, and the pitfalls of going too far out of balance as a result. But we didn't look at the intensely practical value of that new oneness with all creation. The inner changes and simple satisfactions of personal communion with Deity would seem to be reward enough for your seeking, but there is a whole new dimension of good as well. A major change in *you* begins to show itself little by little as you come back to live and work in the mundane or everyday working world. The mystic experience in some unknown manner amplifies the Psycho-Cosmic Power within your being. From the moment of your first contact with Cosmic Reality, your ability to reach the PCP attunement is magnified, thus increasing the quality and quantity of the energies you are able to focus on any of your life's problems.

You become not only a personal ambassador of Deity to his creation, but also a highly efficient channel for the delivery of the PCP energies to individuals and groups in need. In a very real sense your PCP abilities are like a physical muscle. They are strengthened with exercise and intelligent usage, and they tend to atrophy or fade if held inactive for very long. You have a tremendous new power to achieve, but it will stay powerful only if you use it—*and share it with others.*

How to use the power of the spoken Cosmic word

With this new power, there also comes a special new responsibility for the spoken Cosmic word. In perfect oneness with God, Cosmic Good, your word is the word of God and therefore the law of the universe! *In the beginning was the Word, and the Word was with God, and the Word was God. . . . And the Word was made flesh and dwelt among us. . . .* (John 1:1 & 14.) Remember your PCP is now greatly amplified. One friend of mine got a tremendous shock from a short-tempered misuse of the power. He was studying practical uses of PCP in a somewhat frivolous manner and discovered that his spoken command directed at the control mechanism of a traffic signal would invariably cause the signal to change in his favor. For several weeks he practiced this little "game," more or less oblivious to the inconvenience he may have caused other drivers. Then one day as a car cut too close in front of him, he disgustedly cried out, "Oh, drop dead!" His words had about the same effect as a sharp blow to the head of the other driver with nearly disastrous consequences. His remark after telling about this was:

> Al, I never realized the magnitude of this power, or the awesome responsibility that comes with it. If you could have seen the expression on that driver's face—I'll *never* forget it! I know now that I can never use this power strictly selfishly or in a burst of temper again.

Here's how a good woman from New England used PCP to help a friend in need,

> The *light* works just wonderful. The A & C case was brought to court last Friday. C is a very devoted man

—of his kind there is only one in a million—I just couldn't see him get hurt. His chance of keeping the office was one in a hundred. With all my heart I wished that C would be allowed to keep his office he recently opened, which A was trying to close on him. While everyone was in court, I held my hour of meditation. I was sending the pure spiritual *light* to the Judge and the *light* of prosperity to C. It was wonderful news when the session was over. C was allowed to keep his office, and I gave thanks to this wonderful help. I know the light is real.

Use your Cosmic Word Power regularly, but wisely. The best possible safety factor when directing the PCP energies to a specific problem or situation is to demand that they bring *the highest good to all people concerned.* Thus you will receive your good. Often the best solution that our little finite minds can develop is so far inferior to the Cosmic's answer that it would be better for us to do nothing than to enforce an error on our friends or loved ones. Use your power for the good of everyone you contact, but *use it with wisdom and guidance from the higher realms of life.* Claim your continuing growth and personal development daily!

You are properly discharging the responsibility of your PCP energy only if you use it to attain maximum personal Cosmic growth and accomplishment. The aggregation we call mankind is only the sum of the growth and accomplishments of *individuals.* As a species we can accomplish nothing! But as a group of *individuals* united in teamwork and striving to attain the maximum potential of each through the cooperative striving of all, we can take our rightful place as the *wise, omnipotent, and benevolent workers of God on this planet.* Your most important contribution is your own personal growth and success. Use your PCP daily to grow to a high peak of expression. Then if it takes a change of career to go farther, don't hesitate!

You're never too old for a new career

We were in correspondence with a 67-year-young man who is about to become a father for the first time. He was concerned with the purchase of a home—the first he has ever owned! You might wonder what kind of a cave he lived in for the first 65 years of his life, but that doesn't matter one bit. There is only *now* to accomplish! This homely example is important because it shows that successful changes can be accomplished by "little" people.

It's easy for a "great" man to change his career at any point in life. Many popular Generals have retired from active service to become President of the United States. From the first General-President, George Washington, to our most recent, Dwight Eisenhower, our history is full of soldiers turned statesmen. Even well-known actors have turned to the political arena, as Senator George Murphy, and Governor Ronald Reagan. And other important military men "retire" to run large and successful businesses. These are accepted by most people as exceptions to some kind of a rule that says, you're stuck where you are for the rest of your life. *Don't you believe it!*

There is a refreshing trend found in the growing national statistics of Masters and Doctors degrees being earned by students over the age of 50. Now that you are acquainted with Psycho-Cosmic Power, it's your personal responsibility to set a positive example. The same power one man used to bat a driver in the head and change traffic signals can be amplified by your positive desires to accomplish good!

You no longer have an excuse! Things like, "I'm too old," or, "I don't have the education for it," or, "I'm from the wrong race, background or ethnic origin," don't count at all anymore. *The PCP energy doesn't know or care if you are black, white, yellow, blue, or green; or if you're Jewish, Mohammedan,*

Buddhist, Christian, or Zoroastrian. And it doesn't care whether you have a Ph.D. in Psychology or a bare third-grade education! It will work for you! And it is your glorious duty to use it. In truth it is the Supreme Deity's *Will* that you use it!

The Supreme Deity's Will is your ever-increasing expression and accomplishment

Traditional religion makes a great thing about God's will. Remember the old saying, "I'll see you in church, God willin' and the creek don't rise?" Somehow this poses God's will as a kind of restraining force which may plot to thwart our own little plans. Like the Hindu idea of *Karma,* the Christian concept of *God's Will* can be totally defeatist if applied without mature judgment. But without judgment we are capable of producing little more than chaos anyway! So let's apply our judgment to understanding the true nature of God's Will. What must God desire for His creation? Isn't it fullness of expression? Isn't it growth toward ever more perfection of form, thought, and action?

It was necessary to spend a whole chapter on turning tragedy to triumph. It's true that the Cosmic universe may occasionally slap our hands, even as we may slap the hand of our tiny child—not in anger, but to teach a lesson that seems to get through in no other way. What are life's most intriguing pleasures to you? A new Cadillac, a bonus of half a year's salary, a lovely new home, a mink coat, your name in Who's Who, watching your child grow up into something special— any of these may bring momentary pleasure, but they soon remind us of the old Hindu warning, "The fruits of success turn to ashes in your mouth."

That isn't a defeatist crying out that it's no use! It's an injunction to all of us to keep our Cosmic perspective. The acquisition of *things* only breeds the desire for *more things.*

And even the vicarious achievement of growth through one's offspring must lead to demands or desires that are "unattainable." The only true satisfaction is the warm inner glow that comes from personal growth and accomplishment. And even that is dynamic in nature! You can't can it or bottle it to store it up for the future. But you can insure a steady supply by intelligent striving to make something better out of the raw material you call Myself. As you follow a balanced program for self-development and unfoldment, you will feel regular improvement in your oneness with Cosmic Good and an ever growing inner certainty that you are living in accord with God's will.

Now we must pause and be sure we have outlined a truly balanced program for your unfoldment. Certainly we have covered material, financial, and social aspects in earlier chapters. And we can be content with the spiritual seeking of Chapter 16. There is only one element missing. One more thing that will complete the plan and wrap it into a comprehensive whole. This seems to bring us into tune once more with the concluding chapters of my two previous books.

A balanced program to insure your continued Cosmic growth and development

Let's open this section by quoting a paragraph from the final chapter of *Helping Yourself with E.S.P.*:

> Balance is necessary even for spiritual growth and achievement. The ancient occult teachings tell us that we should strive in three specific areas if we would attain balanced growth. They are: (1) work for personal growth and progress, (2) work for the progress of your school, and (3) work for the progress of all mankind. Your progress is inextricably bound up with the progress of all life on this planet. You provide the best spiritual growth for yourself when you strive

also for the good of mankind through the vehicle of some organization whose aims and beliefs are consistent with your own.

This thing called *balance* is very elusive indeed. Modern science is terribly out of balance on the material side. Great scientists have brought us a vast fund of new knowledge about the *material manifestations* of God, though they might prefer to call it something else. And even the new science of Parapsychology is stilted and cold in its approach—seeming to be so limited by socio-academic pressures that it tends to define away the very object of its study. Meanwhile, Religion as a whole has gone merrily along asking thinking men to accept ancient legends on *faith alone,* and decrying the growing numbers of agnostics among our physical scientists. In order merely to maintain its existence, religion is evolving. It is bowing to the "facts" of life presented by modern science, and adjusting its teachings as best it can to be reasonably compatible with contemporary thought.

Science and religion must be reconciled if man is to progress spiritually and thus avoid total annihilation by atomic holocaust. I discussed this in the final chapter of *The Miraculous Laws of Universal Dynamics* from which we will borrow a few lines:

> There is a significant opportunity for a few people to make an unusual contribution to the advancement of mankind by bringing to fruition this link-up of science and religion. The union is inevitable; it is simply a matter of time. But think of the millions of seekers who could be saved from untold suffering if this merger could be consummated fifty or a hundred years sooner than it would by the present groping process! . . . .

A program for your Cosmic advancement

What we "know" today is as a drop in the proverbial bucket to what we should know. If there is anything really impressive in today's world, it must be the contemplation of the gaping voids in our knowledge. Filling the void between science and religion promises more real good for the progress and well-being of mankind than everything that has been accomplished since the Master Jesus put aside His physical body to go on to the Father's many mansions.

You may be working and praying for mankind through some "school" or organization already. I sincerely hope you are. There is no element of competition in these endeavors, since all are working for the common good. If you have no group of your own, or if you have a little extra time to give a push to something new, I invite you to use your PCP to enhance your personal growth by contributing to the force behind this coming merger. Let's do it in three simple steps:

1. Visualize a physical focal point. A "campus," complete with offices, conference rooms, healing rooms, laboratory equipment, digital and analog computers, thinking rooms, a large meeting place, a magnificent library, and perhaps living quarters. Then add a staff of free-thinking researchers in Cosmic Truth whose motto is *RESULTS*. Picture, with PCP power, their widely divergent backgrounds and interests, all contributing to the progress of the whole toward amassing such a *mountain of positive results* that neither the Scientific nor Religious community can ignore or deny. Herein lies your own advancement.

2. Make the PCP attunement. Use the mantra, *Om, mane padme, hum,* while mentally claiming your oneness with the primal Cosmic energy of the universe. Feel your oneness reaching a peak of mystic power and joy, then speak your word confidently as the law of the universe, and it shall be done according to your Cosmic Understanding.

3. Affirm:

I trust in God with all my heart and He directs my growth in the Christ Idea of Cosmic Good. He is giving birth and growth

to an effective organization to unite religion and science in a living, vibrant organism for the upliftment of mankind that includes me, now. Thank you, Heavenly Father, for this perfect gift of Cosmic Unity to your earthly children.

For your own personal results, let me quote once more from *The Miraculous Laws of Universal Dynamics:*

> According to the law of attraction and repulsion, the act of striving to bring a new beginning to mankind assures you of a new *personal beginning.* Accept it and start another round of evolution on the higher level. The peace that passeth all understanding is yours as you consciously cooperate with the evolutionary process. Enjoy it! Share it! Rejoice as you see all mankind moving upward along the great spiral of growth.

Strive to apply the simple truths you have read in this book to every aspect of your daily living. According to your *application* it must be done unto you. *Live in the Cosmic Light,* always.

Points to Remember from This Chapter

1. Your PCP is now greatly magnified. Take care to use it only to bring the *highest good to all.*

2. Age is no obstacle to a new career. There is only the eternal *now,* and its opportunities are unlimited for daily manifestation.

3. The "Will" of the Creator of the Universe is always your ever-increasing expression, fulfillment and accomplishment of good in your daily experience.

4. Personal Cosmic growth is the only sure source of happiness. Attain it by striving for the growth of yourself and all mankind.